Black Film/White Money

Black Film/
White Money

JESSE ALGERON RHINES

RUTGERS UNIVERSITY PRESS
New Brunswick, New Jersey

Library of Congress Cataloging-in-Publication Data

Rhines, Jesse Algeron.
   Black film / white money / Jesse Algeron Rhines.
      p.   cm.
   Includes bibliographical references and index.
   ISBN 0-8135-2266-8 (cloth : alk. paper). — ISBN 0-8135-2267-6
(pbk. : alk. paper)
      1. Afro-Americans in the motion picture industry—United States—
History.   2. Afro-Americans in motion pictures—United States—
History.   3. Afro-American motion picture producers and directors—
United States—History.   I. Title.
PN1995.9.N4R52   1996
384´.8´08996073—dc20   95-33932
                                                              CIP

British Cataloging-in-Publication information available

Contents

Acknowledgments

The essence of culture is artful response to the power distributions, or political realities, in which people are enmeshed. This book reflects a struggle between art and politics played out both inside individual African Americans and within African America.

Back-breaking labor has most ardently expressed Africa's coerced interaction with the white world, but it is through culture that African Americans have most ably responded to this coercion. While ineffective as a weapon against modern armaments and organization, culture has been used by Blacks to reinterpret both external and internal oppressions and render them tolerable. This tolerance is inherent in the conclusion that Blacks' survival in the West is itself reason to celebrate despite continued mass suffering. Artistic expression assuages the emotions jarred by military, economic, and political subjugation. The blues, for example, was an artistic response to the powerlessness of African America in the post-Reconstruction period. Most Blacks, individually and collectively, chose life and cultural expression over the mass death a more militant response might have ensured.

My mother, Mrs. Julia Marie Watson Rhines Steptoe Barbour, a dancer, poet, painter, and government worker who raised twelve kids (brats), gave us specific instruction in how to see and weave through the political realities imposed by the white supremacy under which she was raised. But this instruction we inherited vicariously by watching Mother switch to her "white voice" on the telephone, or seeing her and either the Rhines, Steptoe, or Barbour husband exclaim in wonder if a Black person appeared on television or in a movie. I interpreted these as exceptionally emotional experiences for my mother because she would invariably curse the way whites stood "on Negro throats" soon thereafter. A severe lecture for all the brats on how to survive despite the family's inadvertent poverty, complete with examples of Dwight Eisenhower and other poor people who'd made it, soon followed. My mother gave me artistic appreciation, intellectual curiosity, fear of emotional expression, "backbone," respect for principle, and a worldview based in the lived experience of poor African America. I thank her for all of these.

It was not until my second year in the twelfth grade at Coolidge that I connected art with politics. I was already a photographer, of sorts, but Wendy Wilson asked me to help her start a Black Students' Union. Her Ph.D. in anthropology has taken Wendy to Africa now, but that one request probably set the course of my life to this point.

Once at the Yale Summer High School, to which Dirky Kinard and Ellen (j'ai-b) Bond of Howard University's Upward Bound Pre-College Program sent me, Jim Elston became the first white guy I had much respect for. In his class, student discussion on any and every subject was loud and open. Jim read my papers with great interest and gave valuable advice that demonstrated respect for my way of thinking. Farouk helped me with photography and taught me how to drive a stick.

Late the next year, Arthur D. Smith, Director of Yale's Transitional Year Program, browbeat me about continued bad grades. I worked hard, but there seemed to be a language barrier between me and what my instructors were saying. It reminded me of my white seventh-grade science teacher who implied I lied about feeling a class demonstration's electric shock because I described it as rapid basketball dribbling up my arm. Smith got on my nerves then, but it was his words that took me back to Yale's graduate school ten years later.

Having finished college at Antioch's very left-wing Center for the Study of Basic Human Problems, then having the honor to work for Berkeley, California's Congressman Ronald V. Dellums left me fairly unprepared for the significantly more right-leaning culture of UCLA's Department of Political Science. In D.C. I was also in the Communication Core of the SNCC-run Center for Black Education, which was neither left- nor right-wing. UCLA's Professor Steven Krasner, though very witty and curt, talked with me at length and read rewrites of my papers. I thank him for that.

I shot very few photographs in Los Angeles, but once back in

New Haven I lived and worked at Umoja Extended Family, a community outreach house started by Yale students. I photographed lots of Umoja events and the kids we worked with. While on the legislative staff of the city's mayor, Frank Logue, I started U-SKATE, an Umoja rollerskating business run by and for the kids. Once enrolled in Yale's brand-new Master's in African American Studies Program, I was happy to be back at a school located near a Black community. (Westwood had just been too, too white for me!) I learned a tremendous amount as teaching assistant for Dr. Gerald Jaynes's Political Economy of Urban America class. Robert Ferris Thompson and Sylvia Boone's (RIP) African Art History and Robert Foltz's African Politics classes prepared me well to lead an Operation Crossroads, Africa group to Mali. I must thank them and Dr. Wendell Bell, my M.A. thesis advisor, for their encouragement and support.

Although I decided to broaden my focus from Blacks to interethnic conflict at Yale, I was unable to find a suitable program until I saw Dr. Ronald Takaki, founder of Berkeley's Ph.D. program in Ethnic Studies, on *The Today Show* in 1989. Though he was very soft-spoken, I knew on meeting him that Takaki was a hard case. Pleased as I was with *For Global Pluralism*, an exhibition of photos I shot in the United States, Quebec, Hong Kong, Japan, South Korea, Mali, Martinique, and elsewhere, Takaki was about scholarship, period. In New York City I'd been working closely with Warrington Hudlin of the Black Filmmaker Foundation since 1983, so I was glad Berkeley's program had Dr. Mario Barrera, a political scientist and filmmaker. Takaki and Barrera co-chaired my dissertation committee, and Professors Terry Wilson and Pedro Nogeurra were committee members. Dean Margaritta Melville, assisted by Ms. Linda Manly, was extremely helpful in getting me money to live on while I did research and writing in New York. I regularly mailed Takaki and Barrera dissertation updates and taped their phoned-in progress evaluations. Both they and Dr. Margaret Wilkerson, of the African American Studies Department, sent me job listings. I job-shopped and shopped my dissertation to publishers simultaneously, finally landing first a publishing committment then a job, at Rutgers University Press and the Department of African and African American Studies at Rutgers Newark. I thank Berkeley's administrators and faculty members for providing kindness as well as outstanding intellectual and professional support.

My editor, Leslie Mitchner, guided me, not always so gently, but lovingly, through the process of making this a book accessible to a broader-than-academic audience. I must thank my older brother, John Porter Rhines, my colleague at *Cineaste*, Richard Porton, and my copy editor, India Cooper, for reading, commenting on, and editing various versions of the text. *Cineaste* was also very kind in making photographs available and allowing my colleague John Fried to provide me assistance. Finally, Dr. Wendell Holbrook, chairman of my department at Rutgers, was most understanding when I took ill in late 1993. I thank him, the Newark campus deans, my students, and our staff at Rutgers for continuing intellectual stimulation and all the comforts of home.

Black Film/White Money

Introduction

Like any large, intricate, decentralized enterprise, the Hollywood film industry operates in an environment of uncertainty where many important external, nonindustry forces are beyond the control of industry operatives. National economic and political forces—for example, the Great Depression—can have a devastating effect on movie industry profitability. Rarely are individual persons directly responsible for changes in structures that are global, national, or even industry-wide in scope. Yet one individual may be particularly adept at understanding, predicting, or manipulating structural change in favor of his or her chosen goal. It is those companies and individuals able to adjust to and take advantage of new circumstances which external, structural forces create that are able to thrive.

There are also forces of competition within the film industry itself that have a business-wide, restructuring impact. Such innovations as the close-up, cross-cutting between scenes, the film projector, sound-to-picture synchronization, and modern blockbuster marketing techniques all caused major changes in the structure of the Hollywood film industry. Internal business dynamics such as increases or decreases in ownership of various aspects of the film process by a single company, often called vertical integration, have had direct impact on overall industry structure and the ability of former out-groups to gain new access.

Since its inception, the Hollywood film industry has been greatly influenced by both external and internal structural change, and so has the involvement of African Americans within it. In fact, many of the individuals credited with advancing the cause of Black filmmakers have been less creative than prescient, effective manipulators of circumstances. Oscar Micheaux, Dr. Martin Luther King Jr., Melvin Van Peebles, and Spike Lee, for example, are persons whose

1

real talent lay in their ability to locate and exploit particular, temporary imperfections in both national and industry-wide political and economic structures from which they and, later, others were able to benefit.

To date, four important eras of structural imperfection have affected entree of African Americans into the feature film industry. These structural periods are the silent film era, the Depression and sound film era, the post–World War II period, and finally, the blockbuster/independent distributor period.

In the silent film era, D. W. Griffith brought cross-cutting, close-ups, and epic scope together to create the first feature film, *The Birth of a Nation.* Oscar Micheaux responded to the racist tenor of Griffith's film and launched his own cinematic career. The second era is marked by the Great Depression and the major film companies' use of sound-on-picture synchronization to reverse a slump in ticket sales. The early sound period presented a perfect opportunity for these companies to exploit white people's stereotyped image of Black people as naturally rhythmic; in the 1930s, many Hollywood films featured singing and dancing Negroes.

The third period is unusual because a single individual, Adolf Hitler, appeared as the central catalyst for massive, global political and economic structural changes. Some of these changes, though largely external to African American communities, directly concerned African Americans. The National Association for the Advancement of Colored People (NAACP), Dr. Martin Luther King Jr., independent American filmmakers, and others were able to exploit these changes in the interest of the civil rights movement. Liberal and independent filmmakers were further aided by structural changes within the Hollywood industry forced by a federal government suit against Paramount Pictures for antitrust violations. This suit and post–World War II changes in the global political economy are the conditions responsible for African America's increased access to feature filmmaking.

In this third period the Hollywood industry was also forced to respond to internal structural changes caused by the advent of television and by a new white liberalism, government-enforced desegregation, and Black militancy. These characteristics were almost

Oscar Micheaux
*(Schomburg Center for Research in Black Culture, New York Public Library, Astor,
Lenox and Tilden Foundations)*

nonexistent before the war. Just after the war white liberals and independents produced anti-white-supremacist films such as *Intruder
in the Dust, No Way Out,* and *Guess Who's Coming to Dinner.* Gordon Parks became the first Black person to direct a Hollywood film,
The Learning Tree, in 1969. By the late 1960s, industry cash flow
problems, liberalism, and Black militancy allowed Melvin Van

D. W. Griffith (*seated, center, with hat and stick*) directing,
surrounded by his production team *(Cineaste)*

Peebles's *Sweet Sweetback's Baadasssss Song* to inaugurate the
short-lived "blaxploitation" era.

The fourth period is marked by the 1986 release of Spike Lee's
She's Gotta Have It. Although blockbusters such as *The Godfather*
and *Star Wars* had brought the Hollywood industry out of financial
crisis, in the late 1970s their tremendous cost had also reduced the
number of films produced annually. Dependence on blockbusters
initiated an industry-wide shortage of film product going to theater
owners. It is this structural crisis that ushered in an era when the
children of Black baby boomers gained significant control behind
the motion picture camera.

However important large, impersonal structures may be, "down
here on the ground" real people must find opportunities, make
choices, and take chances. It must be remembered, however, that the
opportunities, choices, and chances are all conditioned by the
political-economic structural environment. Statements by Julie
Dash, Spike Lee, Reginald Hudlin, and other directors, as well as
critiques by journalists and film scholars, indicate three intersecting
areas these new Black filmmakers consider most important: (1) film-

making as a business (financial profitability), (2) filmmaking as artistic endeavor, and (3) filmmaking as a tool of socioeconomic development (Black artist and businessperson social accountability).

While none of these concerns is exclusive to Black film production, all three areas are stood in relief when issues of race are applied. With respect to financing, for example, most, if not all, of the new Black filmmakers believe that the "fact" that they are Black influences their ability to obtain film financing. Even film content and artistry have tremendous racial implications, since films by and/or about Black people employ a disproportionate number of African Americans both behind and in front of the camera. And, with respect to social responsibility, what motivates the frequent public allusion to Black filmmakers' works by journalists, social scientists, and politicians not normally concerned with motion pictures? Walter Cronkite, for example, perhaps America's most respected journalist, included Spike Lee—not just clips from his films—beside white political philosopher Andrew Hacker, political activist Jesse Jackson, former U.N. ambassador Andrew Young, and NAACP Legal Defense Fund attorney Elaine Jones in a televised 1993 analysis of the recent sociopolitical trends in African America. Note, however, that Martin Scorsese, nearly all of whose films are about crime among Italian Americans, is rarely, if ever, on news investigations of Italian American crime syndicates. Wayne Wang, whose tender films critique the Americanization of Chinese Americans, is not enlisted to expound on illegal immigration from China. Why was Lee, a self-styled artist who admits of no sociopolitical expertise, included among Cronkite's commentators?

Race seems often to be a determining factor where nonwhite filmmakers' goals dovetail with the goals of Anglos and other whites in decision-making positions. This interaction between race and filmmaking processes may be an outcome of deeply held ideas on the value and structure of relations between different races. While the new Black filmmakers openly admit to fears and skepticism derived from their perceptions and expectations of hostile, discriminatory, or condescending treatment by white film professionals, white political scientist Andrew Hacker says what his research indicates might undergird white financiers' racial ideas:

(*Left to right*) Grace Blake, Ayoka Chenzira, Julie Dash,
and documentarian Pearl Bowser *(Grace Blake)*

There is a fear of Africa. A fear of the United States becoming
"Africanized." That this will somehow pull us down from our
European origins. From the kind of civilization that white
people have built up over the centuries. As a result we are willing to integrate Hispanics, Asians. We draw the line on people
of African origin.[1]

Despite its significance, however, race is not the primary concern of Blacks in the modern film industry. Theatrical feature films
are, first and foremost, commercial ventures. John Izod, head of Film
and Media Studies at the University of Stirling, says, "Profits have
always, from the earliest days, been the primary objective of the
American film industry."[2] From the standpoint of the movie business, the main goal of any feature filmmaker, regardless of race or
gender, is making money. However, there is also no doubt that because they are not white, Black men and women are generally relegated to the margins of the film industry.

It is commonly estimated that despite being only 12 percent of
the U.S. population, and despite the demeaning portrayal of Blacks
in many American films, African Americans comprise one-third of

the paying audience for motion pictures. The NAACP itself estimates total industry revenues at $4.6 billion "with Black moviegoers making up over 25 percent of box office ticket sales."[3] A primary characteristic of a wholesome economic system is that money spent by consumers be invested locally to improve the conditions lived in by those spenders. Ayoka Chenzira, writer, director, and producer of the independent film *Alma's Rainbow* (1993), noted the importance of this in stating that she prefers to film in Black neighborhoods because even the mom-and-pop shops and local hardware store make money when film crews eat lunch and buy various items needed during a shoot.[4] Yet while *House Party*, *Do the Right Thing*, and *Alma's Rainbow* were shot largely in Black neighborhoods, because in 1995 there were fewer than ten Black-owned movie theaters in the entire country, and because most Blacks see movies—even Black movies—in suburban multiplexes, not in the inner cities where they live, it is almost impossible for Black people's admission fees to benefit their communities. Thus, at a time when more Black films are released than perhaps at any time in history, and when economic conditions in Black America (best symbolized by a Black unemployment rate more than twice that of white America) are worse than in 1960, significantly less than one-quarter of the $4.6 billion spent by African American moviegoers helps to improve their living conditions. In fact, the structure of film distribution and exhibition creates a net outflow of cash from Black neighborhoods. A wholesome economy is not a drain on its constituents. After nearly a hundred years, race remains a hugely important factor in getting African Americans employed, particularly behind the camera.

Chapter 1 Distribution, Production, and Exhibition

Distribution has dominated the Hollywood production-distribution-exhibition cycle since the industry was broken up by the Paramount Consent Decree. The fact that it controls large numbers of the industry's products, the films themselves, is the main thing that gives distribution power. A film production company usually caters to a particular audience segment with a small number of directors and creative people committed to a particular product style. Steven Spielberg's Amblin Entertainment, for instance, is a production company known for using high-cost special effects, fast action, and larger-than-life, white American, male principal characters; its productions are aimed at a white male audience aged midteens through midtwenties. Production companies may make one, three, even ten films per year, but any company will be ruined quickly if a high percentage of these productions fail at the box office.

In contrast, exhibitors try to own as many screens as they can fill to attract a wide audience to their theaters. Their goal is to show as many films as they can get that will attract the largest possible number of paying customers. A film that will encourage repeat viewing by customers who speak favorably about the film and bring friends is an exhibitor's ideal.

Producers depend on distributors to get their films to theaters and to advertise them. Exhibitors depend on distributors to supply them with enough films to keep their screens filled twelve months a year. Placed centrally between these two business arms that have invested millions of dollars in a film's production or in theater construction and facilities, the distributor is in an ideal position to manipulate the entire industry.

The majors are primarily film distribution companies, not film production companies. Although the list has changed over time, the major Hollywood studios include 20th Century Fox, Paramount, MGM, United Artists, Warner Bros., Columbia, Universal, and Disney. By financing the production of films, these large companies ensure that they will have a product to distribute. Exhibitors base expansion of facilities on prediction of a marginal increase or decrease in the number of films distributors supplied the previous year. Essentially, what a distributor does is (1) convince an exhibitor that showing a particular film will be profitable, (2) entice the public to pay to see the film, (3) deliver a print (copy) of the original film to the theater owner, and (4) collect a portion of the box office receipts taken in at the theater.

However, the fact that public tastes are so fickle and unpredictable gives the distributor a great deal of room to maneuver. First of all, producers are people who raise money to finance the vision of directors, who frequently view themselves as artists rather than businesspersons. They do not know theater owners in far-flung cities and nations around the world. They know nothing about buying advertising space in newspapers or on television to market their productions. The director-as-artist is dependent upon the distributor, who is strictly business and, some say, does not care if the profit comes from the movie or from the popcorn sold at the theater.

There is no guarantee a film will attract an audience, so producers and directors negotiate distribution fees on a film-by-film basis. This is called selling the film. Exhibitors must also negotiate the amount they will pay the distributor to rent the film and how long the rental arrangement will be in effect. Everyone tries to get as much as he or she can, but distributors have the greatest leverage, because they know all the theater owners around the world and can pick and choose where to show a film. Distributors also know all the filmmakers around the world—in fact, filmmakers often seek out and design their stories to attract specific distributors—and can pick the ones they believe will attract an audience. Large distributors even have in-house producers who find promising directors and supply them with company funds to make their films.

Of course, distributors want to extract the greatest possible revenue from every picture.[1] Film scholar Gary R. Edgerton says that, to this end, distribution companies have devised rules of operation that benefit exhibitors and others who work with them and punish those who do not.[2] These "rules" include, for example, semicoercive "blind bidding": an exhibitor is forced to show a movie from the distributor's library which the exhibitor has not seen, but which is known to be a "dog" or "low grosser," in order to have the opportunity to show a film expected to be a "big grosser."

In Hollywood, the real money is in distribution, and distributors must keep new films in release to satisfy the voracious appetite generated by thousands of screens around the world running ten, fifteen, even twenty hours per day, seven days per week. Not all of these films are expected to be of high quality. Distributors pick up or finance low-cost "B" movies to forestall competition and support their position as suppliers. Many of these, as well as quite a few expensive "A" films, not only fail to make a profit but actually lose money at the box office. Therefore, distributors must make lots of money on successful films to survive the bite of the more than infrequent dogs.

By the late 1940s, the distribution arm of the industry dominated the production studios and owned so many theaters that the U.S. government itself forced structural change by suing Paramount Pictures, Inc., for antitrust violations. The suit alleged that Paramount constrained competition through vertical integration. The "Big Eight" major production-distribution studio companies—Paramount, Metro-Goldwyn-Mayer, RKO, 20th Century Fox, Warner Bros., Universal, United Artists, and Columbia—were putting all the producers, distributors, and exhibitors still independent of them out of business. Between 1934 and 1937, "95% of all pictures shown in the first-run metropolitan [movie] houses of each of the majors consisted of the releases of the eight companies," who together owned 70 percent of theaters in the ninety-two largest U.S. cities.[3] The result of the suit was the Paramount Consent Decree of 1948, which led to the majors, while admitting no guilt, divesting themselves of their interests in the industry's exhibition arm, the movie theaters, and of long-term contractual control of talent such as actors and directors.

The advent of television also cut into distributor revenues. But it was the networks, rather than independent stations, that mounted real competition, because they had enough ownership in all parts of the television business to exert control on a national scale. As ABC, NBC, and CBS produced higher-quality programming, by the mid-1960s, 90 percent of the less wealthy local stations received much of their programming from the networks. The networks proved powerful political rivals as the majors tried first to enter the field of television program distribution and then, in the 1970s, to attack the networks with a lawsuit alleging activities prohibited by the Paramount Consent Decree. The studios lost this suit, but by the mid-1970s the networks had new enemies, including President Richard M. Nixon, who considered their news reporting biased against him. UHF emerged to compete with the networks' VHF format, and cable television was sanctioned by the Federal Communications Commission. Real competition was now at the networks' door.[4]

Though weakened by television and the 1948 Consent Decree, and reduced from eight to six (MGM, Paramount, RKO, Warner Bros., United Artists, Columbia)[5] in the 1980s, the majors were still the most potent force in the American feature film industry. Independent producers, distributors, and exhibitors remained in direct competition with the major studios for production financing, access to channels of theatrical release, and a share of box office proceeds.

Exhibitor revenues are based upon the number of screens owned. Traditionally, revenue augmentation meant purchase or construction of single-screen theater buildings consistent with expectations of the number of films likely to be available from distributors. After World War II, film releases averaged around four hundred per year. Increased film distribution must have been predicted for the late 1970s, however, because by then the film exhibitors were multiplexing, that is, placing more than one screen in a single theater. However, in the 1970s the majors' production actually decreased; they were financing a smaller number of very expensive, "high-concept" films called blockbusters. In the same period, the number of exhibitor screens increased 10 percent.[6] When, between 1972 and 1975, the majors cut back production by 36 percent, exhibitors formed the Exhibitors Production and Distribution Cooperative

(EXPRODICO) with the intention to pool their money to produce their own films.[7] But the individual theater owners would not invest jointly. Many opted instead to go it alone and only invest in films they controlled. EXPRODICO failed for this reason and was dissolved in 1979.[8] It was replaced by the Theater Owners Film Cooperative, whose president, Tom Patterson, said:

> I think the major problem with EXPRODICO was that they were looking to exhibitors to get the money. Now it's true that some of the large circuits invest in film, but by and large exhibitors are not film investors. You see, the major problem is if you own a film, then you put it in your theater to pay it off, and then it bombs, you lose not once but twice. You have no income on which to write it off . . . The way we kicked this program off is that we made a contract with a group of Canadian investors who have agreed to supply us five films a year over a ten year period . . . Fortunately . . . most of the films today are made independently. If you can provide the financing and the play-off of the film, you can get most any producer in the business.[9]

Thus, in the mid-1970s, both the major distributors, who wanted to produce only blockbusters, and the exhibitors, who were expanding their exhibition space, turned to independent film producers to supply new product. The narrow focus by the majors on blockbusters did not preclude their picking up and then distributing films created by independent producers to satisfy exhibitor demands. In the 1970s, independents filed suits against the big distributors. The majors were alleged to have forced up the cost of production so high that an independent would likely have been forced to seek major distributor assistance at very disadvantageous terms. The majors accomplished this by attempting to "maximize the viewer/cost ratio by producing a smaller number of blockbusters . . . rather than by producing a larger number of lesser movies."[10]

By the early 1980s, screen expansion, combined with a reduction of film properties from the majors, meant that exhibition capacity outstripped properties to exhibit. The 1980s saw Cineplex becoming the dominant exhibition force in both Canada and the U.S. Yet *American Film* magazine observed in the mid-1980s, "Even the mighty Cineplex has trouble getting enough product to fill its screens." This asymmetry between product supply and product demand was an internal structural condition that provided opportunities for small, independent distributors to market the films of the new, young, often film-school-trained directors who were ready to take advantage of the new structural environment.

A 1983 *Variety* article entitled "Hollywood Prod. Labor in a Boom Season" indicated the extent of recent independent producer success. It noted that for behind-the-camera jobs 75 percent of the members of some unions were working—a jump of 15 percent over each of the two previous years. The same article said that independent productions "jumped dramatically in the U.S. this year, almost by two-thirds over 1982. At the same time, productions by the Hollywood majors this year remained pretty constant." Many of these pictures, however, were not shot in Los Angeles and were made nonunion. In the actors' and writers' unions unemployment rates were still 90 percent and 80 percent respectively.[11]

Distribution is the greatest obstacle to broad-based success for African American feature filmmakers, film crews, and film cast members. From the early twentieth century until the present, the lack of enthusiasm that distribution companies, the overwhelming majority of which are controlled by whites, have shown for handling films controlled by Blacks has meant a paucity of Black entrepreneurial and employment success in the Hollywood film industry.

Chapter 2 The Silent Era

It is generally acknowledged that William Foster, through his Foster Photoplay Company, produced the first three all-Black films. These were not features but silent shorts: *The Pullman Porter* in 1910, *The Railroad Porter* in 1912, and *Fall Guy* in 1913.[1] The Foster films depicted Blacks in slapstick humor where a character might first slip, get his head stuck in a barrel, and then be spanked by another Black person wielding a wooden plank.

Blacks were featured prominently in white productions much earlier than this, however. On his Kinetoscopes, which generally showed unedited, nonnarrative documentations of everyday life and allowed only one viewer at a time, in 1895 Thomas Edison featured Black West Indians dancing, bathing, and coaling ships. In 1898, still before film editing was possible, Edison presented *The Colored Troops Disembarking* and later *The Ninth Negro Cavalry Watering Horses*, in which Black troops marched and carried weapons. However, once cutting between scenes allowed a narrative or story line in film productions, Edison and other white filmmakers ceased showing images of African Americans in uniform carrying guns and began making them the butt of jokes and depicting them as cowards or simpletons. In *The Watermelon Contest* he featured "four grinning Negroes" who "wolfed melons" and "spat seeds at will."[2] This presentation of Blacks as "coons," or human objects for viewer amusement, continued. In 1904 Edison presented *Ten Pickaninnies*, in which "a group of nameless Negro children romped and ran about while being referred to as snowballs, cherubs, coons, bad chillun, inky kids, smoky kids, black lambs, cute ebonies, and chubbie ebonies."[3]

Edison initiated mass film viewing with the introduction of the large-screen projector in New York City on April 23, 1896. Less than one month later, on May 18, the U.S. Supreme Court formally sanctioned "Jim Crow" segregation by promulgating its anti-Black, "separate but equal" doctrine in *Plessy v. Ferguson*.[4] Born in the same year, racial segregation and mass film viewing are siblings if not forever squabbling fraternal twins. They have grown up together for nearly one hundred years. This is a paradox of the race issue and the American film industry: while segregation inherently limits a film screening's audience, film producers, distributors, and exhibitors attempt to attract the largest possible audience.

The NAACP began criticizing the depiction of Blacks in white film productions in the 1910s, first with *The Nigger* in 1914, then with *The Birth of a Nation* in 1915. An organization of educated Blacks and whites, started in 1909, the NAACP grew to be the largest, longest-lived, and most well known specifically antisegregation group in America. In the decade following its founding, numerous lynchings of Black men and women combined with the advent of World War I to cause large numbers of southern Blacks to migrate north. Southern agriculture became mechanized as white farmers sold out to large farming enterprises and moved to southern cities. These sales ended the sharecropping and debt peonage systems that had tied Blacks to southern lands since Reconstruction. When Blacks tried to find work in the southern cities, however, whites challenged them with increased lynchings and general refusal of work.

As these events occurred in the South, northern industry grew alarmed as war in Europe reduced emigration of poor white Eastern Europeans who had been the basis of an expanding industrial labor force. Rather than halt expansion, industrialists recruited unemployed Black southerners. Thus, while lynching pushed, the promise of jobs in industry pulled Blacks north. It is this environment that underlies creation of *The Birth of a Nation*. For southerners like Griffith, the idea of free Blacks, no longer tied to rural areas, demanding jobs was abhorrent. His film tells whites how to handle such a menace to society: repression by groups such as the Ku Klux Klan. Woodrow Wilson, a southerner and president of the United States, saw the film before its release and endorsed its message. W.E.B. Du Bois described Wilson's administration as the opening of "a period lasting through and long after the World War and

Protest of a showing of *The Birth of a Nation*, 1947 *(Schomburg Center for Research in Black Culture, New York Public Library, Astor, Lenox and Tilden Foundations)*

culminating in 1919, which was an extraordinary test for their [African Americans'] courage and a time of cruelty, discrimination and wholesale murder."[5]

The Birth of a Nation spurred a rebirth of the Ku Klux Klan. Ten days before its opening in Atlanta, Georgia, Imperial Wizard William

Joseph Simmons publicized the film's premiere and led a Thanksgiving Day erection of a fiery cross on Stone Mountain. He then placed a Klan recruitment notice next to the film's ad in the *Atlanta Constitution* newspaper. As Blacks moved north during the world war, *Birth* was used repeatedly as a propaganda and recruitment tool by Klan sympathizers in Chicago, New York, and other cities as well. Maxim Simcovitch attributes the film's rhetorical power to two factors: uneasiness in the Black belt as African American troops returned from war, and white riots precipitated by the increasing Black migration north.[6] One of the film's last scenes shows the repression of African Americans as mounted, armed Klansmen force Blacks to stay at home on election day.

African Americans were not the only group attacked or demeaned by white filmmakers. In Cecil B. DeMille's *The Cheat* (1915), which became "the talk of the year," Asians are depicted as vile and treacherous.[7] The sexual exoticism of one character, a Japanese art collector, includes the branding of lovers; audiences screamed for him to be lynched. Thomas Cripps notes, however, that Blacks were the largest nonwhite group by 1914, when Adolph Zukor and others were moving to California to build the movie business, and therefore "the social struggle to shape cinema into a democratic art form became theirs."[8]

The 1915 release of *The Birth of a Nation,* which the film's director, Griffith, proclaimed was, in part, designed "to create a feeling of abhorrence in white people, especially white women, against colored men," was well received by the industry.[9] The nascent film distribution companies, on learning of "prolonged applause" at a private, pre–New York release screening before a house packed with "opinion makers," were quick to approach Griffith. Louis B. Mayer, later of MGM fame, offered him $50,000 and a fifty-fifty split, after covering costs, for distribution rights in New England, excluding Boston. "Since Mayer wasn't yet in the financial league of the bigger distributors, the guarantee had to be hastily raised from Mayer's dependable group of investors—nearly all of them mercantile Jews in Boston who seemed less concerned about being tainted by the movies than they were about making a profit."[10] *Birth* has been called the world's first blockbuster motion picture, and Mayer alone made half a million dollars from this one deal.[11] Protest against this film brought Blacks and whites together in the first major contest over racial discrimination in the motion picture industry. *The Birth of a Nation* also inspired production of the first Black feature, *The Birth of a Race*. That famed Black educator and spokesman Booker T. Washington and his adversary W.E.B. Du Bois attempted cooperation in this production makes this film's social, if not political, moment apparent.

Du Bois, the first African American to receive a Ph.D. in sociology at Harvard University, was a founding member of the NAACP, which at the time was considered radical on the issue of race relations. As editor of the NAACP's magazine, *The Crisis*, Du Bois opposed the more conservative course, now called accommodation, urged by founder and president of Tuskegee Institute Booker T. Washington, a nationally acclaimed orator who was on perhaps better terms than any other African American with white leaders of industry and government. The conflict between Du Bois and Washington is well known. Du Bois urged Blacks to agitate for classical education and political rights. Washington scoffed at the thought that training in Greek or Latin could help the majority of Blacks, who were overwhelmingly uneducated and rural, and urged a focus on industrial education and economic development.[12] Anthropologist John Brown Childs says that opposing views on the value of capitalism for Black people's development was the essence of the argument between Du Bois and Washington. Washington saw modern industrial capitalism, represented by his benefactor, steel magnate Andrew Carnegie, as inherently antiracist. As progressive capitalism expanded from the North, the racist South would be "overwhelmed and transformed." In contrast, Du Bois saw racism as an inherent part of capitalism's global expansion. Rather than join the capitalists Du Bois sought "a free territory in which to develop an effective resistance."[13] Despite their mutual acrimony, however, the NAACP and the Tuskegee group (Emmett Scott and others negotiating on behalf of Booker T. Washington) came a hair's breadth near working together to counter Griffith.

Both the NAACP and the Tuskegee group protested *The Birth of a Nation*, as did African American brothers Noble (a bit actor at Universal Pictures) and George Johnson, whose Lincoln Motion Picture Company was incorporated in 1916. Although these groups "barely knew of each other, so wide had the diaspora spread them," they considered producing a film in response to *Birth*. And their reasons for making this movie were quite different. The Tuskegee Institute group was after a response to Griffith's film for racial uplift purposes alone. It wanted to use financing from whites in Chicago. The Johnson brothers wanted to make the picture themselves to boost their reputation as a production company focused on a Black aesthetic. And the NAACP wanted one of the major studios to produce a film that would counter Griffith's movie.[14]

There is no evidence that either Du Bois or Washington had demonstrated interest in film production prior to release of *The Birth of a Nation*. Their intention in this filmmaking venture appears to have been strictly motivated by political interests. Cripps says that Du Bois and Washington "shared the common goals of producing movies with black investments in the plot-lines, black characterizations with humane dimensions, dramatic conflict based upon the facts of American racial arrangements, and a conscious effort to make the tools of the filmmaker speak to black needs." The NAACP's "scenario committee," including W.E.B. Du Bois, began the preproduction process by contacting Universal Pictures' Carl Laemmle in May of 1915. Universal screenwriter Elaine Sterne, a white woman, was to help the committee shape the production of *Lincoln's Dream*, "a celebration of black progress."[15]

Approaching Carl Laemmle to handle this "race movie" was not an insignificant thing even in 1915, although a mature understanding of the movie business clearly reveals its naivete and tremendous temerity. Why would perhaps the biggest and most profitable film production studio of its day make and distribute a picture clearly at variance with the desires of its audience? Today, Black filmmakers have learned that big, established companies are risk averse. Small, independent distributors are more likely to take a chance on an untried idea. Laemmle himself had recently been an independent, warring against what he called "the Trust," a loose association of East Coast "older white Anglo-Saxon Protestants [led by Thomas Edison], who had entered the film industry in its infancy by inventing, bankrolling, or tinkering with movie hardware: cameras and projectors. For them, the movies themselves would always be novelties."[16]

In 1909, Laemmle began making his own movies after a few years of fighting the Trust in distribution. His innovation was luring prominent stage actors to the screen and raiding his competitors' acting stables to create such film "stars" as Mary Pickford and Florence Lawrence (formerly known to the public as "the Biograph Girl"). In 1913, Laemmle's salary at the Independent Motion Picture Company of America, which he helped form, was over $100,000 a year, and he had a personal fortune of over $1 million. Internal bickering and mutual raids against the Trust and other competitors led Laemmle to reorganize the company under the name Universal. When the dust settled in 1915, Universal was opening America's most modern and efficient studio, and Laemmle was receiving press as a virtual unknown who had become "King of the Film Renters."[17] After such a battle, Universal was not the company to ask to challenge a status quo it had fought so hard to create.

Universal did, however, make an offer to put up $60,000 for the filming of *Lincoln's Dream* if the NAACP would come up with $50,000. But individual NAACP members themselves turned out to be risk averse, preferring, Cripps says, to be anonymous partners unwilling to chance losing their own money. The NAACP was never able to raise more than $10,000 from outside sources, nor would it, despite Elaine Sterne's efforts, commit its own resources to making the film. Sterne began looking for a new backer and found her way to Booker T. Washington and his personal secretary, Emmett J. Scott. After some months of correspondence and trips between New York and Alabama, Universal withdrew its offer of matching funds, and Scott and Washington interested Edwin L. Baker of the Advance Motion Picture Company of Chicago in filming Washington's autobiography, *Up from Slavery*, as a response to *The Birth of a Nation*. Upon Washington's death that same year, this project was given up, and Scott once again turned to *Lincoln's Dream*, this time calling the film *The Birth of a Race*.[18]

This three-hour feature, though completed, was a hodgepodge of financial interests and chicanery. Many people with various interests controlled the filming, but few of those interests centered on uplifting the Negro race. *The Birth of a Race* remains such an embarrassment to present-day African American film scholars that they often refuse to show it in their classes and rarely request its presentation at Black historical film festivals. Cripps says that "only two small flaws" in the arrangement engineered between Scott and Baker caused the problem: "Scott had unwittingly given Baker the right to sell his interest to a third party unbound to Scott's conditions, and in his haste to avoid an overbearing white company Scott had taken up with a Lilliputian." Baker disguised his company's financial weakness under "periodic stockholders' newsletters." By spring 1918, the Selig Polyscope Company had spent $140,000 to finish only half the shooting. When Selig and others backed out of the project, Daniel Frohman of New York stepped in to complete "a vast biblical sequence which bore no relation to Selig's footage," and Scott realized he and his Black partners had lost production control. "More Negro footage was left in the cutting room when the producers again shifted emphasis to take advantage of the rising war fever." Soon thereafter, Baker told *Variety* that the film "would not be about the Negro at all and that Scott was no longer a scenarist."[19]

George and Noble Johnson's Lincoln Motion Picture Company did not participate in the production of *The Birth of a Race*. Lincoln, first under the Johnson brothers, then under Clarence Brooks (who later played perhaps white feature filmmaking's first Black professional, a graduate of Howard University's medical school, in John Ford's *Arrowsmith* [1931]), made films that "tended to emphasize black pride and consciousness, and were often explicitly political."[20] The company's productions avoided direct portrayal of Blacks in the worst of economic conditions, preferring to show them beating the odds in the white-dominated system. Their 1917 *The Realization of a Negro's Ambition* showed a Tuskegee graduate leaving the South and getting an admirable position in California from the white and otherwise racist owner of an enterprise as a reward for saving the man's daughter. Eventually the graduate makes his own fortune, marries the woman of his dreams, and lives a happy life, the equal of any white family's.[21] *The Trooper of Troop K*, also produced in 1917, attempted to build race pride "by showing that Afro-Americans were allied militarily with Anglo-Americans" as part of

Pershing's reprisal raids against the Mexican revolutionary Pancho Villa.[22] This film was quite a hit with Black audiences: "At Tuskegee 1600 students exulted in its quality and its black theme. In New Orleans it ran in Black and white houses and in many dates drew 'record breaking crowds.' In Omaha [Noble] Johnson essayed his first premiere, using Negro lodges, bands, and well-heeled black bourgeoisie."[23] Although profits never were sufficient to finance their next picture, the Johnson brothers went to great lengths to avoid the financial problems suffered by Emmett Scott.[24]

The Johnson brothers made great efforts to continue their independent business but were denied the outside capital and financing so important to their white competitors.

> By 1917 with only two pictures in release they had exchanges and press agents in most of the ghettos of America. Their most imaginative tactic outstripped white Hollywood in its search for a profile of its audience. Exhibitors received a survey sheet asking for house size, ratio of black and white patrons, names of the local black press, thematic and topical preferences, and most striking, a request for a comparison in audience response to Noble Johnson's work in Lincoln and in Universal productions.[25]

This latter point may have wreaked havoc on Lincoln's attempts to get financing from wealthy Blacks such as hair-care-product empress Madame C. J. Walker, bankers, and Robert L. Vann of the *Pittsburgh Courier*. On seeing his drawing power, Universal undermined the Black company's profit potential by threatening to stop employing Noble Johnson in its films unless he ceased starring for Lincoln.[26] Noble Johnson was in an increasing number of white productions after 1917, and in 1927 he was the only Black actor featured in at least four films: As an "Apache" in *When a Man Loves*, Uncle Tom in *Topsy and Eva*, a ship's cook in *Vanity*, and an exotic in *The King of Kings*. In these early days of cinema, the huge white companies knew there was a market, both African and Anglo American, for films featuring African American stories and characters, and they saw African American producers as skilled, competent, yet severely undercapitalized competitors for this market.

To what extent did Laemmle at Universal favor white competitors over Black competitors? While he was perfectly willing to strangle Lincoln, a Black competitor, and place a high matching fund requirement against production of Scott's Black counter to *The Birth of a Nation*, Laemmle's white competitors considered him extremely generous.

> Even competitors testified to Laemmle's basic decency. Thomas Ince, an important producer/director in the movies' early days, lost his studio in a fire while he was shooting an epic entitled *The Battle of Gettysburg*. There seemed no alternative but to shut down production, until Laemmle generously offered his own facilities and telegraphed, "Do not charge him a cent for them." "He is the only man in the industry who would do that," Ince said in what was probably an accurate assessment of the internecine business in those early years.[27]

Ince, a white businessman, was certainly greater potential competition for Laemmle than either Emmett Scott or Noble Johnson. There may or may not have been more personal relations between Laemmle and Ince, but in any case, racial preference seems a valid reason for whites to prop up white competitors while they destroy Black competitors.

Noble Johnson's last picture for Lincoln was *The Law of Nature* in 1917, but Lincoln continued limited production with *A Man's Duty* in 1919 and *By Right of Birth* in 1921.[28] In the 1920s, there was an abortive exchange of letters between the Johnson brothers and a new, but very active, filmmaker named Oscar Micheaux with a thought toward combining African American filmmaking efforts.

The end of World War I saw no improvement in American race relations. Returning Black soldiers, who had expected their participation to be appreciated by their country, instead were still relegated to Jim Crow living and were often beaten in the street by whites. This is the climate that launched the person known as the father of African American cinema. Beginning with silents in 1918, Oscar Micheaux made and distributed from Harlem forty-four films in thirty years. Twenty-four of these were features.[29]

Micheaux was more entrepreneur than artist, and his employees sometimes called him underhanded. His solution to the problem of distributing his films was to "bicycle," or hand carry individual prints from theater to theater across the nation in early spring. He would show his movie to a house manager, along with the script for the next feature to be made. Sometimes he would be accompanied by his star actors and actresses. Micheaux would then begin to haggle with the manager for rental fees and length of play in the theater in an attempt to secure an advance against the film's return. By late spring Micheaux would be back in New York to film the script as its producer, director, and often even cameraman. He would edit during the summer, and by fall he would be on the road again bicycling his film from theater to theater and promoting it as he went along. "And the system was successful. Even with limited, generally low-income audiences, he was able to make a feature film every year for two decades without a grant, subsidy, or monopoly, an achievement subsequent filmmakers would envy."[30]

Micheaux dealt with "lynching, 'passing,' race purity, prostitution, gangland life, and he even made a jungle film."[31] He wrote at least ten novels in his lifetime, the first of which, the autobiographical *Homesteader*, was the model for his first feature film in 1919 by the same name. In 1924, *Body and Soul* featured Paul Robeson in his first role. This was also the last time Robeson would work for a Black director. Another silent film, *Marcus Garland*, in 1925 "burlesqued the Black Moses, Marcus Garvey, who had made himself president of 'The Republic of Africa' before being convicted and sent to jail for mail fraud in 1925."[32] Many films by Oscar Micheaux, *Underworld* and *God's Step Children*, for example, depict upwardly mobile Blacks working alongside or instructing their less successful brethren in an environment nearly devoid of white people. Micheaux designed Black environments both separate from and equal to those of whites, and his films often had a decidedly Black bourgeois nationalist subplot.

There is no indication that the creation of "art" was Micheaux's objective. Film historian Donald Bogle says that "Micheaux well understood the mass imagination, and by catering to its wants and needs he was able to survive and become successful . . . Learn from the masses; then teach them" was his philosophy.[33] Micheaux's objective was to "make a difference." In fact, Oscar Micheaux was a race man—the title given *by Blacks* to those men who worked to uplift African America as a race.

Oscar Micheaux's films demonstrate that he was an African American bourgeois, like Du Bois and Booker T. Washington—that is, a supporter of capitalist entrepreneurship—and an activist African American nationalist politico. *Underworld* shows both Du Bois's talented tenth, the 10 percent of the Black population Du Bois advocated receive a full, liberal education, and Booker T. Washington's bootstrapping economic and industrial development programs in action. *Underworld* protagonist Paul Bronson, though a naive waif, is clearly a member of the talented tenth. Educated in the European classics, he even recites poetry, as did Du Bois. When the film opens, Paul has his degree and is not risk averse, as demonstrated by his taking an additional chance on LeRoy, the classmate we see him confront for having duped him before. Later, Paul even says he shoots crap on occasion. He condemns the numbers racket, however, instructing the audience from a practical vantage point: one's probability of success with numbers is low. The woman Paul is with at the film's end, Evelyn, the college dropout, is also business minded and is trying to start her own beauty parlor.

Both *God's Step Children* and *Body and Soul* also show Black attempts at economic development. The evil Reverend Perkins of *Body* extorts booze from a small-time Black "social club" proprietor, and *Step Children*'s educated protagonist, Jimmy, is intent on buying and developing a farm adjacent to an already successful farm owned by an uneducated Black farmer. In this film, Jimmy even breaks the land-buying process down for viewers, explaining mortgages and other technical matters.

Where Noble Johnson and William Foster had ended up working within the established Hollywood studio system, Micheaux remained independent of the major studios in terms of financing, story input, and distribution and marketing assistance. However, Micheaux would not remain independent of white financial support as the Depression era set in.

Creation of the seminal film of the early twentieth century, *The Birth of a Nation*, occurred between two larger political and

Poster for Micheaux's *Underworld* (Schomburg Center for Research in Black Culture, New York Public Library, Astor, Lenox and Tilden Foundations)

economic contexts, the mechanization of southern agriculture and the First World War. Griffith's film was a response to the former event, while the war provided Blacks the opportunity to escape his call for greater repression by migrating north. In response to *Birth* more Blacks began making films. Oscar Micheaux emerged as a leading African American producer as the silent film era drew to a close.

Chapter 3 # Depression and
World War II

Improved conditions for Blacks as a group, even within the film industry, are normally the result of structural and political economic changes affecting white America. Historian Ronald Takaki says that, as the Great Depression began, "in 1930, the majority of blacks still lived below the Mason-Dixon Line, growing cotton as sharecroppers and tenant farmers. Their livelihoods crumpled along with the stock market: cotton prices had dropped sharply from 18 cents per pound in 1929 to 6 cents in 1933. That year, two-thirds of the blacks cultivating cotton only broke even or went deeper into debt."[1] These worsening conditions for Blacks did not cause a sympathetic response from white Americans. Rather, as Blacks moved to southern cities in search of work, angry unemployed whites confronted them shouting, "No jobs for niggers until every white man has a job!" "Niggers, back to the cotton fields—city jobs are for white folks."[2] In fact, newly unemployed whites leapt at the chance to snatch menial jobs they had once refused from African Americans still employed.

Nor did Roosevelt's New Deal present early proof of federal good intentions toward Blacks. Political scientists Dona Cooper Hamilton and Charles V. Hamilton report that while both the National Urban League and the NAACP supported the espoused universal ideology and intent of the proposed Social Security Act of 1935, both groups had difficulty supporting the initial legislation because it did not cover the nearly two-thirds of the Black labor force composed of agricultural and domestic workers. Before the Senate Finance Committee, on February 9, 1935, NAACP attorney Charles H. Houston stated:

The NAACP regrets that it cannot support the Wagner Economic Security Bill (S. 1130). It approached the Bill with every inclination to support it, but the more it studied, the more holes appeared, until from a Negro's point of view it looks like a sieve with the holes just big enough for the majority of Negroes to fall through.[3]

Not even Blacks' liberal allies were forthcoming on protection for the poverty-stricken agricultural workers. The NAACP's Roy Wilkins reported to colleagues what executive secretary Abraham Epstein of the American Association for Old Age Security said of the Wagner Act:

Mr. Epstein, who has known of the work of the Association [NAACP] for many years and who is familiar with most of the problems of Negroes stated that colored people were in a tight place as far as this legislation was concerned, but he did not see that there was anything that could be done about it. *He said frankly that he was interested, first, in social insurance and that he did not see how we can solve the Negro problem through social insurance; in other words, there are realities existing with respect to Negroes and whites in this country which no program of social insurance can undertake to correct.*[4]

At this juncture, W.E.B. Du Bois responded to the NAACP's continued focus on integration as the ultimate solution to the ongoing crisis among African Americans by resigning his position as editor of the organization's *Crisis* magazine. Edward Peeks observed that integration

eschewed self-determination for Negroes as a group in a pluralistic society made up of many groups—despite all the integrationists' glibness about "the melting pot." Du Bois wanted genuine group recognition for blacks—not token and individual recognition—throughout American life. . . . He wanted the NAACP to lead the way by setting higher goals in the political and economic realms. Joel Spingarn [a white NAACP supporter] expressed dissatisfaction with the integrationist NAACP program as the Depression deepened. But his was not half the concern of other NAACP board members who, first and last, were committed to a bare-bones policy of legislating integration.[5]

In opposition to the "noneconomic liberalism" of an integrationist approach, Du Bois proposed "a third path." Blacks should establish economic cooperatives to foster their own economic development. According to Peeks, in the co-op plan

> Blacks could raise their own food, build houses, produce raw materials, such as cotton and tobacco, and process them for market through co-ops. The vast Negro labor pool could be harnessed directly to all these activities, even to transferring skilled workers to wherever they were needed and teaching such "additional skills as can easily be learned in a few months." Negro-owned and Negro-controlled enterprises could compete in the general economy "if [Negroes] bought in large quantities and paid cash, instead of enslaving themselves to white usury."[6]

Du Bois argued that it was "impossible that a segregated economy for Negroes in the United States should be complete," but it might go a long way toward the "great ends" to which the Negro was moving.

In opposition to the Du Bois plan, the NAACP called for "the building of a labor movement, industrial in character, which will unite all labor, white and black, skilled and unskilled, agricultural and industrial." By 1933, the Depression had led management to use Blacks as strikebreakers, and the white labor unions had countered by reaching out to Blacks. The United Mine Workers brought Blacks into the union by using Black organizers and stressing equal pay, regardless of race. The Committee for Industrial Organization (CIO) announced its policy as "one of absolute racial equality in Union membership." After enrolling Blacks, who constituted 12 percent of Ford Motor Company's work force in 1941, the United Auto Workers obtained wage increases and union recognition.[7]

While racism had by no means diminished, competition between northern white management and labor unions spurred renewed northern migration of Blacks and, Takaki says, "led to a national political realignment; increasingly, [Blacks] became an important force in the northern states that possessed a large number of electoral votes. . . . [T]o attract black voters, New Deal policy makers [began] to address the needs of blacks. . . . In the 1936 presidential election, according to George Gallup, over three-fourths of northern blacks voted for Franklin D. Roosevelt, who had been promoted among them as the second 'Emancipator.'"[8]

Micheaux was nearly the only independent African American filmmaker to continue successful production through the Great Depression. The Depression's tragedy was exacerbated for Black filmmakers by stiff competition from more affluent, white American companies better suited to weather the economic downturn. In addition, the new technology of sound-to-picture synchronization suddenly threw up new cost barriers that pushed the creation and distribution of competitive pictures beyond the financial abilities of most independent Black producers.

The 1927 release of *The Jazz Singer* demonstrated the economic and technological viability of sound-picture synchronization, and all the major studios went after the new technology. Soon four thousand Vitaphones, only one of the sound systems in development, were being produced each week. Rewiring a theater for sound cost up to $20,000, totaling $12 million of installation in 1928 alone. White distribution/production companies often owned the theaters where their films were shown and were wealthy enough to finance such refurbishment. This was not the case for Black producers, who often negotiated each showing at individual theaters. The struggling Black companies could barely finance silent film production. Thus, although Micheaux's sound features were almost a miracle of entrepreneurial determination, they were not successful competitors with white productions even for an African American audience. He filed bankruptcy in February 1928. Film scholar Mark Reid says that Micheaux's problems resulted from faulty distribution systems, censorship rulings, print costs, the high cost of sound technology, and the centralized management of Harlem theaters. After 1929 an alliance with white Harlem theater owners Leo Brecher and Frank Schiffman allowed Micheaux to continue making films.[9] He did not release his first sound feature until 1931—three years after the technological boom began.[10]

One of the main attractions in many white productions of the early sound era was Black music, singing, and dance. And, film historian Donald Bogle says, "the roar of the cash register reflected their ability to entertain." Normally these African Americans were presented in a restricted sociocultural and political perspective: for example, down south on an antebellum plantation. In almost every 1930s movie featuring Blacks—*Hearts of Dixie* and *Hallelujah*, for example—filmmakers tried to "maintain the myth that Negroes were naturally rhythmic and natural-born entertainers . . . Even as Bessie Smith cried the blues in *St. Louis Blues*, she was at heart the entertainer."[11] Ed Guerrero says of the 1938 *Jezebel*, "All the black parts of the film are time-honored stereotypes that legitimate the slave system and serve as devalued or comic counterpoints to white roles. . . . [Blacks] stand silently fanning or waiting on the master class, with no thoughts or articulation of their own."[12] Black music and dance were used in white films because they attracted white audiences. In the early sound recording era many white companies recorded traditional African American vocal and instrumental performances as examples of what they called the highest quality of human musical achievement.

Sound-on-film brought Hollywood jobs to many singing and dancing Negroes and drew Black audiences who wanted to see and hear other African Americans in high-quality, big-screen productions. Yet these were not happy times for their image on screen, and even all-Black features, such as *Stormy Weather* and *Cabin in the Sky*, focused on singing and dancing Blacks wielding switchblades and speaking in the broken English whites associated with Blacks of the South and of slave days. *Hearts of Dixie*, *Hallelujah*, and *The Green Pastures* were only a few of the all-Black musicals, in addition to "cameo" performances of "coon," "mammie," and "buck" roles, protested by the NAACP and other social-political organizations on picket lines, in newspaper articles, and through the courts.[13]

To try to combat these images, William Foster again tried to make features himself, this time with sound, but found little encouragement in Hollywood. He asked Blacks to join together, implying that with the popularity of the Negro voice and sound technology Blacks must use "our great opportunity to show the world what we can do." But by the mid-1930s he was saying that "the Negroes fight me harder than the whites" and complaining:

The white man has fell flat trying to Produce a real Negro show as he has always did. Hearts of Dixie and Hallelujah. the Big Producers are afraid to produce a big Negro Drama. the South will resent it. Boycott their pictures, would throw the Business into Politic. one told me If the Negro want Big Pictures of Negro life of today they will have to produce them themself [sic].[14]

Spencer Williams, who played Andy in the 1950s television comedy series *Amos 'n' Andy*, was active as an actor, writer, and producer for his own and white independent films in the 1930s and 1940s. He directed Midnight Productions' silent film *Tenderfeet*. Then Williams co-wrote and starred in the first all-Black talking film, *Melancholy Dame*, which was directed by the white American Octavious Roy Cohen and released by Paramount in 1928.[15] In 1940, Williams wrote the script and played a detective in an all-Black-cast knockoff of the King Kong clone *Ingagi*, Richard C. Kohn's *Son of Ingagi*.

Many of the all-Black films of this period were produced and directed by whites in independent companies such as the Goldberg brothers' two operations called Negro Marches On, which for ten years made all-Black films, and Million Dollar Pictures. In 1942, the Goldbergs had this to say:

We don't go in a great deal for star names, because a colored performer who's a great hit up North may not mean a thing to our audiences south of the Mason-Dixon Line. All they know is that they want plenty of singing and dancing or drama depicting Negro life in typical Negro spirit. They are wonderful audiences, too; there's nothing sophisticated or cold about them—but they definitely know what they want.[16]

But the Goldbergs' pictures differed from the Hollywood all-Black fare in that they allowed nonstereotypical African American characters and stories. In the early 1940s, Jack Goldberg made *Othello*. The brothers' Million Dollar Pictures produced a typical murder mystery, *Four Shall Die* (1946), with Mantan Moreland and Dorothy Dandridge in a love triangle. This was also the first major independent film company to give African Americans "a substantial amount of control over production."[17] They even had an internship plan

Poster for *Son of Ingagi* (*Schomburg Center for Research in Black Culture, New York Public Library, Astor, Lenox and Tilden Foundations*)

whereby Tuskegee, Howard, and Hampton Institute students were paid the fair wage of $100 per week for principals, $60 for supporting actors. "But the Goldbergs understood that the key to the movie business was distribution and they carefully appraised and mapped out their audience—thirteen million American blacks in about five hundred theaters, plus those at mid-night performances in southern white theaters."[18]

Spencer Williams's own company, Amergro Films, produced *The Blood of Jesus* in 1941 and *Go Down Death* in 1944. But, scholar James Snead says, "the horizontal and vertical monopolization of the film industry by the major studios, combined with the introduction of noted black actors (such as Mantan Moreland, Ethel Waters, and Bill Robinson) into white films, had by the late '40s all but extinguished the early vitality of black independent film."[19] The world was at the brink of a new era, however, in which global events unrelated to movies would force white America to change the way it related to Blacks both in and out of the film industry.

Chapter 4 The Negro Cycle through Blaxploitation: 1945-1974

The end of World War II marked a turning point for African American involvement in the Hollywood film industry. It is important to note, however, that the postwar improvement both in job opportunities for Blacks and in the portrayal of Blacks on screen was a product of the worldwide structural changes caused by the war itself. White Americans, either as a group or as individuals, had not had a spontaneous moral advance that rendered them more kindly toward Blacks. Rather, structural changes beyond individual reach allowed Blacks greater freedom.

After World War II, global and domestic reaction to Adolf Hitler's racist campaigns and destruction of Europe's colonial empire allowed the industry to bring Blacks out of the pastoral South and into the modern world. In fact, America's ascension to global political, economic, and military predominance made it the most watched nation on earth and the focal point of peoples-of-colors' global, anticolonial struggle.

Often this transition to greater white American tolerance of African Americans is said to be rooted in both the militancy of returning African American soldiers and the organizational prowess of Dr. Martin Luther King Jr. Without the radically changed international environment, however, both the veterans' and race leaders' demands might have fallen on deaf ears as they had following World War I. The primary cause of post–World War II civil rights success was not only the federal government's willingness to pass legislation favorable to Blacks but, more important, the executive branch's willingness to enforce laws on the books. This willingness was chiefly the product of external pressure on the American government's hypocritical attempts to combat European colonialism abroad while maintaining colonial domination of Blacks domestically.

In 1935, few, if any, Blacks would have predicted the radical change in white attitudes toward them that occurred after World War II. Although Dr. Martin Luther King Jr. led the postwar movement for civil rights, it would be irresponsible to view the movement's successes as his alone, outside the context of domestic and global pressures. These pressures encouraged high-ranking whites to acquiesce to many of the movement's demands. It is also unlikely that the leadership of any individual African American, however charismatic or morally persuasive, could overcome centuries of white supremacist predilection. Ronald Takaki and others have recently pointed to alternative explanations.

The start of the Second World War indicated little future improvement in African America's living conditions. Takaki says:

> Though blacks fought bravely in the Pacific and Europe, they were defending a democracy that for them still represented a dream deferred. . . . Although they were allowed to fight and die for democracy, blacks were excluded from the defense industry. In 1940, they constituted only 0.2 percent of the workers in aircraft production. . . . Unwilling to wait for employers to open employment to them voluntarily, blacks demanded action from the federal government. At a meeting of frustrated blacks in Chicago in 1941, a black woman called for a mass demonstration in Washington: "We ought to throw 50,000 Negroes around the White House, bring them from all over the country, in jalopies, in trains and any way they can get there, and throw them around the White House and keep them there until we can get some action from the White House."[1]

In the hands of experienced organizer A. Philip Randolph, head of the Black Brotherhood of Sleeping Car Porters, the threat of a march on Washington caused alarm in the nation's capital. Takaki says that officials asked, "What will they think in Berlin?" To quell the threat, President Roosevelt established the Committee on Fair Employment Practices by signing Executive Order 8802. With this the president ordered that "there shall be no discrimination in the employment of workers in defense industries or Government because of race, creed, color, or national origin. . . . Again it is the duty of employers and of labor organizations . . . to provide for the full and equitable participation of all workers in defense industries."[2]

Between 1940 and 1945, more than half a million African Americans fled the South, and whites met them with violence in Detroit, New York, and many other cities. By 1945, African Americans were more than 8 percent of defense industry employees.

In addition to domestic labor, management, and political competitions, post–World War II geopolitical realities, that is, global power politics, were also fundamental to the official change in U.S. racial policy. The formation of the multiracial United Nations in the aftermath of a mighty struggle against Hitler's racist, anti-Semitic ideology forced the United States, as leader of the free world, to make domestic relations between races a reflection of what policy makers urged between nation-states: harmonious, consultative, and mutually supportive. In the spring of 1944,

> [President] Roosevelt himself felt that he could no longer fail to combine publicly the general notion of human rights with the specific principle of racial equality. For this reason he finally announced, "The United Nations are fighting to make a world in which tyranny and aggression cannot exist; a world based upon freedom, equality, and justice; a world in which all persons regardless of race, color, or creed may live in peace, honor, and dignity."[3]

China and other nonwhite U.N.-founding nations demanded that racial discrimination be openly outlawed in international relations, and this finally had domestic impact in white-ruled countries. In the 1945 *Re Drummond Wren* case the High Court of Ontario, Canada, dismissed racially discriminatory real estate covenants, citing the United Nations Charter's human rights and fundamental freedoms articles as justification. Soon, U.S. courts followed Canada's lead, saying that the U.N. Charter required that segregation and racial discrimination be eliminated.[4]

In 1948, the U.S. Supreme Court deemed unconstitutional the Alien Land Law, which prohibited Japanese from owning and leasing land. The Court called the law "nothing more than outright racial discrimination" and "referred to the United Nations Charter as well as the struggle against the racial ideology of the Third Reich."[5]

In 1952, the U.S. attorney general filed a brief before the Supreme Court stating that

> it is in the context of the present world struggle between freedom and tyranny that the problem of racial discrimination must be viewed. . . . Racial discrimination furnishes grist for the Communist propaganda mills, and it raises doubts even among friendly nations as to the intensity of our devotion to the democratic faith.[6]

It was into this postwar race relations context that, in 1955, the young Dr. Martin Luther King emerged in Montgomery, Alabama, to head the Dexter Avenue Baptist Church. While Alabama officials may have seen the local racial environment as little changed from prewar days, the federal government now saw things quite differently. The federal government and much of the national industrial infrastructure had now been conditioned by a number of forces and events—from the northern migration of Blacks to a greatly liberalized international environment—which led them to enforce desegregation. As leader of the civil rights movement, Dr. King "fused together [the] Christian doctrine . . . [of] 'Love your enemies, bless them that curse you, and pray for them that despitefully use you' . . . and Mahatma Gandhi's tactic of nonviolence" to challenge the new national and federal sociopolitical environment and achieve the conservative goals of integration and noneconomic liberalism.[7]

It is impossible to understand the post–World War II opening of the American film industry to Blacks without considering the altered global geopolitical and economic environment in which U.S. government officials operated. The international political structures that had sanctioned or ignored America's racial caste system were undone. Governmental decisions regarding Blacks, such as Truman's desegregation of the armed forces, signaled acknowledgment of these changes. Soon, paying audiences provided support for Hollywood's white independents and liberals, as well as for others farsighted enough to make films reflecting the new racial attitudes forced on white America. However, even bigger changes were soon to come. A new structure of the film industry itself would soon foster greater independence of expression.

Blacks and Movies in the Civil Rights Environment

Halting moves toward liberation of Black Hollywood began in the late 1940s and paralleled developments in the civil rights movement from the integration movies of the sit-in period through the blaxploitation movies of the Black Power period.

The "Negro cycle" films emerged with the sit-ins. These were films produced and directed by whites often newly independent of the major studios and, for the first time, able to shop their ideas from studio to studio. Negro cycle films showed one or a few Blacks struggling in a white world. In the first twenty years after World War II, while Blacks were humanized on screen in white-produced films, there was little change in the racial makeup of film crews. In addition, the subject of films such as *Intruder in the Dust* (1949) and *No Way Out* (1950) was the deplorable way whites treated Blacks much more than the life lived by African Americans. These films took advantage of the new postwar liberalism and pointed white audiences toward acknowledgment and respect for African American rights.

In fact, the first ever nonstereotypical, nonmusical Hollywood film centering on middle-class Blacks in the north did not come until Harry Belafonte and Dorothy Dandridge starred as schoolteachers in *Bright Road* in 1953. Yet, later in the 1950s, the all-Black musical was back with *Porgy and Bess*, starring Sidney Poitier, and *Carmen Jones*, again with Dandridge and Belafonte.

All three of those films were written, produced, and directed by white people and targeted a white audience. Oscar Micheaux died in 1951, and there was no significant movement toward independent Black feature production until Melvin Van Peebles emerged in the politically radical 1970s. The mid-1960s, however, brought more African Americans to the screen, and a different kind. As the attraction diminished of what Sidney Poitier himself called the "one-dimensional, middle-class imagery" he portrayed in such films as *No Way Out* and *Lilies of the Field* (1963), Jim Brown and other Black sport stars found themselves on the screen.[8] In the film *100 Rifles* (1969), Brown and Raquel Welch (portraying a Mexican) sizzled in interracial sex denied Poitier's characters.

Famed *Life* magazine photographer Gordon Parks was the first

Director Gordon Parks behind the camera *(Cineaste)*

African American to direct a Hollywood feature film, *The Learning Tree*, for Warner Bros.–7 Arts in 1969. The film was based upon his autobiographical novel of the same name. Parks made the film for $3 million supplied by Warner Bros. He said, "I had fourteen or fifteen people behind the camera for the first time in the history of films. There was a Black director. The producer was Black. The scoring was done by a Black man. The third cameraman for the first time was a Black man." He went on to say:

> It took a strong young man like Kenny Hyman [of Warner Bros.] to break down all those barriers after all those years. It took one man to say, "We're going to have a black director in America; we're putting up the money. Anything he wants, he has . . . " So when these men, who are heads of studios, say there will be a black director, it can happen, and it can happen overnight. If Kenny Hyman had not wanted me, there probably would be no black directors today, because the minute he did it, everybody felt, "Well, it's happened. We better open up now."[9]

Of course, it was not just the courage of "one man," as Parks contends, that "opened up" Hollywood directing to Blacks. Structural changes had reduced the risk that a Black director of a Black-cast film would flop at the box office. Hyman was perceptive and courageous enough, and the major studios in need of new markets enough (after the Paramount Consent Decree and television crises), that Black directors would be found.

Bad Niggers

The Student National Coordinating Committee (SNCC) originated the term "Black Power," and its leader, Stokely Carmichael, is credited with having first systematically applied the term "internal colonialism" to African America.[10] SNCC, which was originally active in the sit-ins as the integrationist Student Non-Violent Coordinating Committee, sought Black control of the Black community both in rural areas and in urban ghettos. "They rejected the idea of the 'talented tenth' [Du Bois's alternative to Washington's emphasis on vocational training] who would come out of the colleges to lead. There would be no 'talented tenth.' Only the Community."[11]

The SNCC leadership was not decided on the question of land. Some urged the secession of southern states for Blacks. Others urged that Blacks join an African land base. Yet all conceded Black Power meant "the political and economic power and cultural independence of black people to determine their destiny individually and collectively, in and out of their own communities."[12] SNCC also originated the use of a black panther as symbolic of Black empowerment with its Lowndes County, Alabama, Freedom Party. Eighty percent Black, Lowndes County had no Black elected officials, and no Blacks had ever been allowed to register to vote by 1965, yet the newly created, all-Black Freedom Party of Lowndes County pitted the black panther in elections against the State of Alabama Democratic Party's official symbol: a rooster crowing proudly, surrounded by a banner declaring WHITE SUPREMACY—FOR THE RIGHT.[13]

By the mid-1960s, the NAACP and the Southern Christian Leadership Conference (SCLC), led by Dr. Martin Luther King Jr., had lost the allegiance of many young African Americans who were adopting African names and African dress and calling for community control of schools and other public facilities. SNCC's Carmichael openly opposed King's commitment to nonviolence, and the call for Black Power reinvigorated the civil rights movement. Their organization and voting-rights drives inspired creation of Oakland's Black Panther Party and brought poor rural African Americans into the struggle for Black liberation.

Although Gordon Parks's direction of *The Learning Tree* for Warner Bros. marked a milestone in Hollywood feature production, it was Melvin Van Peebles who best captured the new attitude in African America and made most creative use of structural imperfection in the 1970s film industry. Stating that what major studios like Columbia Pictures, which had offered him a three-picture contract, called a little control he called extreme control, Van Peebles dropped the contract to make a "revolutionary" and independent film.[14] Produced for $50,000—the money he had earned as director of Columbia's *Watermelon Man*, a loan of $50,000 from Bill Cosby, and funds from nonindustry sources—Van Peebles's $500,000 production, *Sweet Sweetback's Baadasssss Song* (1970) changed the course of African American film production and the depiction of African Americans on screen.

Sweetback champions a "'bad Nigger' who challenges the oppressive white system and wins," says film scholar Ed Guerrero, "thus articulating the main feature of the Blaxploitation formula."[15] Political scientist and professor of African American studies Charles Henry says of this African American folk type: "From the slaves' Br'er Rabbit and Slave John to the more recent Great MacDaddy, John Henry, Railroad Bill, Dolemite, Shine, and Stackolee, the 'bad Nigger' or black 'bad man' tradition is characterized by the absolute rejection of established authority figures."[16] Sweetback—Van Peebles himself played the role—a sex hustler, is on the run after almost inadvertently saving a Black man from being framed by police. The Black community—and particularly women who screw him even while he is handcuffed—protects him.

Unlike the experience of Gordon Parks with Warner Bros., Van Peebles avoided paying film industry craft union wages by claiming to be producing a porno picture. He also wrote and directed the film

Melvin Van Peebles as Sweetback, *Sweet Sweetback's Baadasssss Song*
(Cineaste)

and composed the music, in addition to playing the leading man. Released through Cinemation, initially in only two theaters, one in Detroit and one in Atlanta, *Sweetback* grossed over $10 million in its first run. This film was so financially successful that Gordon Parks's second Hollywood directing effort also championed a "bad Nigger." This time he was *Shaft* (1971), a private detective who challenged the traditional, white-dominated New York City police system. With a $1.2 million production budget, this film grossed $11 million at the box office.

Parks's *Shaft* and, especially, his son Gordon Parks Jr.'s *Superfly* (1972) refined the blaxploitation formula. Nelson George, who wears many hats, among them *Billboard* magazine writer, novelist, author of the influential *Death of Rhythm and Blues*, and writer/co-producer of three feature films, says that *Superfly*, with a $500,000 budget and $5 million gross in less than one year, "sets the tone for the black criminal as antihero. . . . Where Shaft was a typical detective flick in blackface, *Superfly*'s cocaine dealer was a more romantic, conflicted figure whose slang and clothes cut deeper than *Shaft* into the black community's psyche." From 1971 through 1974, says

George, white-owned distribution companies released on average some fifteen films per year, up to one-fourth of all films in production, featuring Blacks as strong, sexy characters, frequently at war with traditional Euro-American norms.[17] Donald Bogle says these films played on the Black audience's need to see African Americans on screen without answering that need in realistic terms.[18]

Sex, violence, and dope are the hallmarks of the blaxploitation film. In *Coffy* (1973), full-figured Pam Grier sets the female mold as she wields a shotgun in retribution against the gangsters and politicians who hooked her younger sister on drugs. In *Welcome Home, Brother Charles* the Black star's penis takes on a life of its own and, stretching to more than twenty feet long, creeps across rooms to invade the bodies of sleeping women. In *Mandinga*, set during slavery, a white woman visiting a plantation is so aroused at a slave's whipping that she sneaks back to the place where he remains chained, standing with arms and legs outstretched. She seduces him, kissing and rubbing her hands all over his wounded, bleeding body.

But despite the black hipsters and "foxy" women on screen, the blaxploitation period was not an example of African American filmmaking. Much more often than not, whites were in control behind the camera reproducing their own point of view. In fact, of the hundred or so films featuring significant numbers of African American characters and/or an African American–derived story line and produced during the blaxploitation period, roughly 1970 through 1974, fewer than one-fifth were under African American control. Even fewer came from Black-owned production houses, and fewer still were financed and/or distributed by African Americans. Films aimed at an African American audience, featuring significant numbers of Black characters and/or an African American–inspired story line, but controlled by non-Blacks may more properly be called Black-oriented films. Bogle says that "many of the new Black-oriented films were written, directed and produced by whites. . . . Worse, many of the new movies were often shot on shoestring budgets, were badly directed, and were technically poor. The film industry hoped simply to make money by indeed exploiting an audience need."[19] These films were released during the height of the civil rights/Black liberation movement, yet their subject matter of sex, violence, and "super-cool" individualism was the antithesis of what contemporaneous black political organizations, like SNCC, the NAACP, or SCLC supported for Black people; hence the name "blaxploitation," a term coined by *Variety*.

Sidney Poitier, Harry Belafonte, Bill Cosby, Ossie Davis, and other Blacks also produced and directed both comedies and dramas that were not exploitative from the late 1960s through much of the 1970s. In the early to mid-1970s, TAM tried its hand at distribution; Calpenny, E&R, and K-CALB produced African American films; and Woodie King Jr. attempted distribution and production. Ossie Davis, a stage actor who had performed with Sidney Poitier in *No Way Out* and with Sammy Davis Jr. in *A Man Called Adam*, directed a comedic film version of the Chester Himes detective novel *Cotton Comes to Harlem* in 1969. While the film grossed over $6 million, United Artists was unwilling to finance a sequel, and Davis turned to an independent, international project, *Kongi's Harvest*, for Nigerian playwright Wole Soyinka's company, Calpenny Ltd. (California, Pennsylvania, and New York). Soyinka intended the production company to have both U.S. and African components. The distribution companies—Paramount, Warner Bros., United Artists, and Columbia, among others—found *Kongi's Harvest* "too special, too African" for a mass distribution and passed on it. But Davis described the film, which has an all-African cast and was shot in Nigeria, as "a comedy of African politics [which shows] Africa as Africans see it." And this fact, he conjectured, might have been the reason white American distributors rejected it. "Africa without Tarzan may be too raw, too threatening, too strong for their blood," he said, "but that's exactly why we made *Kongi's Harvest.*"[20] After fifteen months of screenings before distributors, TAM, a new company organized by three Washington, D.C., African American businessmen, stepped in planning to distribute "genuine films about black people" rather than "the current wave of so-called black films [which] simply exploit the black moviegoing public by offering black faces in white roles and pretending to offer reality."[21]

Ossie Davis was also instrumental in the creation of New York's Third World Cinema Corporation, which was designed to "produce, in New York City, films and documentaries utilizing talents and providing jobs for blacks, Puerto Ricans, and other minority groups, and to distribute them to motion picture houses and television."[23] This organization trained many of the producers, directors, and other technicians who have crewed films made by Black filmmakers since 1985. However, much of the funding for this group came from the federal government—$400,000 of it from the Model Cities program—and these sums were substantially reduced or eliminated during Richard Nixon's second term as president. Third World Cinema did produce the films *Greased Lightning*, with Richard Pryor under African American Michael Schultz's direction, and *Claudine*, directed by John Berry, a white Jewish American who suffered in the McCarthy era. "The Bronze Barbie Doll," Diahann Carroll, played Claudine, a Harlem domestic worker who has six children and is living on welfare. She falls in love with the garbage man, played by James Earl Jones. The *New York Times* called *Claudine* "a financial and critical success,"[23] and Carroll received a Best Actress Oscar nomination for her work.

Woodie King Jr. and Herbert Danska, respectively producer and director of the winner of the 1970 International Film Critics Prize and the Interfilm Award at the Mannheim Festival, *Right On*, shunned established distributors United Artists and Universal, preferring to appeal directly to the Black audience. In preparation for the 1971 release of this "dramatic visualization of the Last Poets of Harlem" by Concept East New York, Ltd., King concentrated advertising on soul radio stations in New York and on leaflets, flyers, and posters in select neighborhoods, and he used fewer than the customary number of ads in daily newspapers. He previewed *Right On* in Harlem and opened it in theaters on the West Side.[24]

Despite a large Black audience the first week, however, the film did not succeed at the box office. James P. Murray, author of *To Find an Image: Black Films from Uncle Tom to Superfly*, concludes the reasons for this failure are that Blacks, as typical of what he calls the "weekend movie audience," respond poorly to "message" films in commercial theaters and "enjoy leaving their communities to go 'downtown' and be entertained in style."[25]

K-CALB attempted a similar plan in Compton, California, then a middle-class Black enclave near Los Angeles, although it had first

Harry Belafonte (*left*) and Sidney Poitier (*right*) are honored at NYU's
conference "Black Cinema: A Celebration of Pan-African Film," hosted by
Dean Mary Schmidt Campbell (*center*) of the Tisch School of the Arts
(Jesse Rhines)

sought closer ties with Hollywood. Its 1970 film *The Bus Is Coming*,
directed by Wendell James Franklin, who in 1962 had become the
first African American member of the Directors Guild of America,
was made for under $250,000 (including deferred costs). Although
it remained in theaters for only a few weeks, *The Bus Is Coming* did
beat *Shaft*'s early receipts by earning $77,000 after two weeks in re-
lease.[26] This film, which was saved by William Thompson, "a new
distributor recently arrived from the Midwest" who provided finish-
ing costs, played at the 1971 San Francisco Film Festival and went
on to gross $4 million before international distribution.[27] At this
time TAM and Cinemethics International were the only two Black
feature film distribution companies.

Sidney Poitier, Bill Cosby, and Harry Belafonte together acted in,
produced, and/or directed a variety of films between the mid-1970s
and the mid-1980s. *Uptown Saturday Night*, *A Piece of the Action*,
and *Let's Do It Again* are all 1970s comedies starring Bill Cosby and
Sidney Poitier, their director. The post–Civil War western *Buck and*

Ruby Dee and Cameron Mitchell in *Buck and the Preacher*
(Museum of Modern Art/Film Stills Archive)

the Preacher (1972) was produced and directed by Poitier and
starred both him and Belafonte. It tells the heroic story of a group of
former Louisiana slaves on their way to a Black western town. En
route, however, they must fend off plantation owner agents who attempt to force their return south. *Stir Crazy* (1980) and *Fast Forward*
(1985) employed Poitier as director into the mid-1980s, but for reasons to be considered later, the Black movie boom had ended in

1974. Between the mid-1970s and mid-1980s, Richard Pryor and Eddie Murphy were featured as sole Black protagonists among a host of white supporting characters. They were comedians in films normally written, financed, produced, directed, distributed, and crewed by whites. These two men were, independently, the image of African Americans shown on movie screens around the world. *Fast Forward, Beat Street* (1984), by Black director Stan Lathan, which focused on the break dance craze from the Bronx, New York, and the early productions from Doug McHenry and George Jackson at Warner Bros., featuring increasingly popular rap musical artists Run-DMC, were the early murmurs in the post-1985 phase of African American filmmaking.

Expansion of opportunity for Blacks as a group has occurred in the Hollywood film industry, but only when national or industry-wide structural imperfections are evident. For example, after World War II, white America's general sympathy for the civil rights movement allowed Blacks to direct Hollywood films and to play heroic, nonthreatening roles on screen. The Black Power movement allowed Blacks to strike out at whites and to celebrate cultural traits distinct from those of white America. Most of the financial benefits from films featuring Blacks in this period, however, went to the white directors, producers, writers, distributors, and exhibitors. Not until the mid-1980s did an industry-wide structural change occur that allowed Blacks greater access to positions of control behind the camera.

Chapter 5 Blockbusters and Independents: 1975 to the Present

In the 1970s, the major studios had yet to recover completely from the debilitating effects of the Paramount Consent Decree, the advent of competition from the recently invented television technology, and the doubling of film production costs between 1962 and 1972. In the 1960s, the first two difficulties caused a crisis in the industry.[1] Between 1959 and 1970, the majors' combined distribution of four hundred dropped to an average of only 250 films per year. This low supply of films hurt exhibitors.[2] The majors' incomes were declining. To combat this decline they changed their strategies. Mass communications scholars Garth Jowett and James Linton observe that there are two strategic options to making money in the feature film industry: (1) minimizing production costs, that is, making a smaller, more specialized movie, or conversely (2) maximizing potential appeal, that is, making a blockbuster.[3] Blaxploitation films are extreme examples of the first strategy. *Shaft* and *Superfly* were very low-budget features targeted at a very narrow market, the African American audience. Between 1970 and 1974, many white filmmakers made handsome profits from the blaxploitation genre film.

However, says film scholar Ed Guerrero, "when Hollywood no longer needed its cheap, black product line for its economic survival, it reverted to traditional and openly stereotypical modes of representation, as the industry eagerly set about unplugging this brief but creatively insurgent black movie boom."[4] From the mid-1970s through the 1980s, blockbuster after blockbuster was released by the majors. The *Star Wars* trilogy, the *Indiana Jones* quartet, *Jaws I*, *II*, and *III*, and *The Deep* were but a few features with elaborate special effects, shot in exotic locations, and paying stars enormous sums of money. However, the films themselves are not the real story of the majors' phoenix-like recovery in the 1980s. Rather, their success is the product of applied research used to promote these films. Film industry insider James Monaco observes, for example:

> The real secret to Columbia's success in 1977 was not *Close Encounters* at all, it was *The Deep*, a more conventional package, presold by Peter Benchley's novel followup to *Jaws*. It had a couple of stars, some acceptable adolescent sex (Jackie Bisset in a wet teeshirt), and an outrageously racist plot, where not only are the villains all black but they do strange voodoo sex things to our Jackie.[5]

At $31 million from its June opening to the end of the year, it was the sixth-highest-grossing film of 1977. Success was based on the way producer Peter Guber sold it.

Guber spent nearly two years devising *The Deep*'s marketing strategy. First hardcover, then paperback books were published. Magazine excerpts and condensations followed. Publicity on the set was constant, and journalists were enticed with a junket to Bermuda. Guber wrote the gossipy *Inside "The Deep,"* which was full of behind-the-scenes "news." The first printing of this book was 124,000 copies released the final two days before the film's premiere. Since most workers get paid on the fifteenth, *The Deep* opened June 17, 1977. Research told Guber that by now each potential moviegoer would have been hit by at least fifteen print, television, or other media exposures of the film.

Saturation booking of eight hundred theaters, or about 6 percent of total American theaters at the time, opened *The Deep* on the same day. Guber reasoned that getting theaters filled quickly would protect the film from bad word of mouth or bad reviews. Monaco says the theory is to "get in quick, get the money, and get out before the bad news trickles down. . . . A see-through blue-vinyl soundtrack album, a treasure-chest contest at supermarkets and shopping malls, department store mannequins dressed in *The Deep* teeshirts," and products from boat, watch, and cosmetics manufacturers tied the public imagination to the upcoming film.[6] In June, while a merchandising campaign was building steam, for advertising as well as to make money from tie-ins, Guber, the film's director, Peter Yates, the book's author, Peter Benchley, and the stars were on all the talk shows.

Columbia allotted $1.5 million for print and $1.3 million for television advertising. Their objective was for the nation's fifty top markets to receive two and a half billion visual advertising impressions during the month of June. The publicity, marketing, and distribution campaign for *The Deep* set the mold for the modern blockbuster film. Another Columbia blockbuster, *Close Encounters*, used a similar strategy with an advertising budget of half the film's $9 million production costs. "Saturation marketing" and "saturation release" were the keys to blockbuster success. As a result, "distribution's share of the domestic market increased from $500 million in 1972 to $1,215 million in 1978 or 143%, while the gross U.S. box-office figures grew only 67%."[7]

The Mass Audience

The Peter Guber marketing approach is a wonderful example of the operation of the mass audience model. Clint Wilson and Felix Gutierrez, the authors of *Minorities and Media*, describe this model as one in which racial minorities are seen at the margins of a coveted American mass audience where they are ignored not only by those in the movie industry but by other media that seek a mass audience as well. In 1978, Otis Chandler, then publisher of the *Los Angeles Times*, was quoted as saying, "We cut out unprofitable circulation, and we arbitrarily cut back some of our low-income circulation." In 1976, a *Detroit News* editor ordered his staff to "aim the newspaper at people who made more than $18,000 a year and were between the ages of 28 and 40." Such stories, the editor wrote, "should be obvious: they won't have a damn thing to do with Detroit and its internal problems." Wilson and Gutierrez argue that newspapers seek a mass audience at the demand of their advertisers, who want to reach more affluent, now suburban readers. They say that some newspaper circulation strategies were designed to make it "difficult, if not impossible for residents of ghettos and barrios to subscribe to newspapers . . . at the same time they were starting or expanding new editions in outlying areas. The strategies were defended as being based on economics, because the low-income characteristics of blacks and Latinos made them undesirable news-paper readers."[8]

This approach also states that media seeking a mass audience will look for "commonalities" or "themes" to which large majorities will respond. Again, racial minority groups and their peculiar "cultures and traditions" will be ignored or, where used, will be presented so as not to offend the mass audience. Minorities will be pictured as "seen through Anglo eyes," or stereotyped in order to present a "common content denominator" to potential viewers.[9] However, the most effective way to avoid confronting nonwhite peoples is to avoid employing members of nonwhite races as much as possible.

In line with the least-common-denominator approach to reaching a mass, mostly Anglo audience, the majors either avoided depiction of nonwhite domestic cultures or stereotyped individual minority group members throughout the blockbuster period. Use of a fairly uniform, generic cultural environment aids in appealing to the largest audience possible, which since the 1950s has been about 75 percent under thirty with the greater portion between fourteen and twenty-five years old.[10]

American Film magazine reported that in the 240 films released in 1981 there were only a dozen major roles for Blacks. Of all "on-camera parts in the 4th quarter, ten and two-tenths percent went to blacks and Hispanics." Brock Peters, who starred with Gregory Peck in *To Kill a Mockingbird* (1962), stated, "The only leading roles offered to blacks [were] those that support a white lead. There is a false theory that audiences will not go to see a black star unless that star is accompanied by a white counterpart." Yaphet Kotto, who has played significant roles in such films as *The Thomas Crown Affair*, with Steve McQueen, and *Alien*, with Sigourney Weaver, says it's not racism, it's economics: "People want to be involved in fifteen- to twenty-million-dollar movies, and they want their returns guaranteed. So they go for the Redfords, the Connerys, the Brandos. . . . If they ever scale their expectations down and return to modest, low-budget films, they might just turn to me."[11]

Janet Wasko, author of *Movies and Money*, appears to support

Kotto's view that race is not the real issue. She says that the movie industry does not produce pure art or pure communication but, rather, commodities that are produced, distributed, and exhibited under market conditions. Market scrutiny "inevitably" influences who makes films, the type of films made, and the manner of public distribution. James Monaco says investors are more likely to "throw in for a share or two" if, by appealing to a minority audience, a film promises to "make back its investment plus a small profit in a relatively short space of time." So casual a strategy is impossible for the blockbuster, however, because the risks are too high: production and marketing costs of up to $30 million, $50 million, even $100 million demand that research virtually guarantee a market before a film is made.[12]

Jowett and Linton observe that the producer knows that his or her films will be viewed by individuals. But as marketeer, the producer must group these individuals into "diverse 'publics . . . ' for *each specific movie.*" Producers try to routinize actions required to make a profit on new movies by using actors and ideas already proved to attract an audience.

> Faced with [high] uncertainty, moviemakers have generated an implicit philosophy or ideology about movie-making which provides them with an image of their audience and their viewing interests. This "audience image" has tended to narrow the range of subject matter and forms that movies employ, and has caused moviemakers to invoke formulaic approaches and engage in imitations of "breakthrough" successes, in what are known as movie "cycles." As innovations are introduced and the environment changes, the "landscape" of the industry adapts, with the "chameleonlike" majors managing to maintain dominance in the marketplace.
>
> . . . [A]dvertising campaigns [sometimes] cost as much as the actual production of the movie itself, and "some recent marketing campaigns have cost as much as twice the negative cost."[13]

In her book *American Film Distribution*, Suzanne Mary Donahue says that large-scale publicity can so whet public anticipation that "people feel that it is a social necessity to see a film."[14] In recent years even box office grosses are published and touted in advertising to draw further attention to a film. The popular belief, generated by high grosses, that everyone else has seen a movie may make more people feel that seeing it is a social necessity.[15]

The early distribution experience of the 1973 independent film *Hester Street* demonstrates how the majors' preconceptions and risk aversion can miss the opportunities presented by a small film. Director Joan Micklin Silver made this film for only $356,000, but it was very well received at the Cannes Film Festival. From Cannes *Hester Street* sold well in several foreign countries. But in the United States, the film made the rounds of the major Hollywood distribution studios three times and was rejected. When Silver and her husband were informed that the film's black-and-white cinematography, low budget, and ethnic orientation caused the majors to predict a box office failure, they decided to distribute it themselves. Because of the film's success at festivals, some exhibitors were willing to book the picture in a few theaters. When *Hester Street* actress Carol Kane received a Best Actress Academy Award nomination, however, hundreds of smaller exhibitors opened up to it. The picture finally grossed more than $4 million.[16]

Despite such rare stories of success and the general profitability of the blockbuster technique, industry professionals still point out that meeting the public's tastes at a particular time remains a crap shoot. Even big-budget films—*Ishtar* and *Hudson Hawk*, for example—can fail, because the public taste is fickle and what seems a sure bet when shooting starts can be the last thing the public wants to see one year later when the film is released.[17]

The mass audience approach dictates that cultural out-groups will be stereotyped or depicted in ways that will not offend the majority of viewers. John Sayles, producer of such low-budget independent features as *The Return of the Secaucus Seven*, *Brother from Another Planet*, and *Eight Men Out*, who left a prosperous and productive career as a Hollywood writer to become an independent producer, says, "I co-wrote one movie called *The Challenge*, and the director said, 'Well, I know they're all Chinese in the script, but let's make them all Japanese because I can get Toshiro Mifune and who knows the difference anyway?'"[18]

The primary mission of studio heads and those white males re-

(*Left to right*) Writer-filmmaker Nelson George, writer-filmmaker John Sayles, filmmaker Reginald Hudlin, writer Thulani Davis, screenwriter Richard Wesley, filmmaker Warrington Hudlin *(Jesse Rhines)*

sponsible for hiring, and against whom many equal opportunity suits are filed, is to design a homogenized film image that will draw the greatest number of viewers. Ironically, as Monona Wali points out in *Black Film Review*, Hollywood may be missing an opportunity to reap even larger profits. "Commercial cinema also ignores one of the fundamental realities of America today—it is increasingly a multi-racial, multi-cultural society, and the various races and cultures seek to have their images represented in their full and true dimensions."[19]

Since the mid-1970s, as major distributors have reduced the number of films they finance and/or release per year in an effort to release larger-budget films with greater Anglo, mass appeal and a correspondingly greater short-term box office potential, the use of both nonwhite actors and themes derived from nonwhite people has been deemed potentially alienating to this mass audience and therefore avoided or homogenized, that is, depicted in a way distributors project will be nonthreatening to the greatest pool of potential ticket purchasers. From the mid-1970s through the early 1980s, major studio concentration on blockbuster production and mass marketing techniques ended the industry's financial crisis. This focus on so-called high-concept, almost monoracial movies also limited non-white people's access to lead roles, to film production financing, and to channels designed to get film products shown in American theaters. Hollywood executives did not realize, however, that by reducing the number of films released they had provided rare opportunity to a new breed of independent producers and distributors.

Niche Marketing

Independent distributors do not start out competing with the majors. Mass marketing is the furthest thing from their minds and abilities. Independents operate in niche or specialized markets normally ignored or serviced by the majors with "B" or genre films. The market at which a film is aimed is very important, especially for the first-time producer and the small distributor. Astute assessment of the types of productions a particular audience will find entertaining and, therefore, will pay to see is the primary task of the specialized marketeer. In fact, what is entertaining to a specialized market is rarely entertaining to a mass audience.

Genre marketing is the independent distributor's equivalent of the majors' mass marketing technique. Success in this area comes from developing a sustained following for films because of specific attributes, whether or not the film is a critical success. Martial arts and horror are genre categories that have developed such followings. A few of these, *Night of the Living Dead* and *Rocky Horror Picture Show*, for example, have also developed a cult following, which ensures a long-term revenue stream. Certain types of comedies do as well, the *Airplane* and *Police Academy* series, for example. The majors secure a devoted following from mass audiences by featuring big-name actors, stars whom large audiences are inclined to see regardless of the film's quality.

Genre films are not "art" films, however. Art films pose a greater risk for distributors since they present a filmmaker's very personal vision for which no audience has been developed. Early John Waters films fit this category, as do *The Producers*, *El Norte*, Julie Dash's

Daughters of the Dust, Hector Babenco's *Kiss of the Spider Woman*, and, some say, Spike Lee's *She's Gotta Have It*. Art films have a more narrow, less predictable market than genre films and are frequently shorter lived and less profitable. They rarely contain elements intended for, or conducive to, sequel development: for example, *Night of the Living Dead*, an early 1970s release, led to sequels into the 1990s; yet none of the films Spike Lee has produced sequels his first, *She's Gotta Have It*, because they do not use elements developed in his original success.

Barbara Kopple's documentary *Harlan County, USA* is said to be the avatar and the beginning of a wave of late-1970s independent American feature films.

> There are several reasons for this sudden surge of activity. The proliferation of film schools in the late sixties flooded the market with ambitious, often socially conscious, young talents. At the same time, the conglomeration of Hollywood reduced the number of low-budget, "experimental" studio films. Unable (or unwilling) to crack the industry, aspiring filmmakers were forced to create their own opportunities. Movies had achieved a certain prestige as tax write-offs—and, for a time, tax shelters—and, even more important, there was an increasing amount of foundation funding available.[20]

Independent productions of the 1980s differed from films released by the majors both in terms of the amount of money spent on their production and in the way they "imaged" colored people and/or women. Films like *Who Killed Vincent Chin?*, *El Norte*, *Do the Right Thing*, and *Desperately Seeking Susan* all challenged the dominant feature film industry's portrayal of nonwhites and/or women and were deemed "socially conscious" for this reason. Independent filmmakers like Peter Wang or Wayne Wang (they are not related) and the Hudlin brothers do not want to make the same kinds of films Hollywood is making. Hollywood's preference for already proven audience-getters is, generally, not in accord with a social consciousness that seeks to overturn the views on race, class, and gender most white American audiences have traditionally supported at the box office. Examples of the views these new filmmakers wish to express are: female independence in thought and action is good; cross-class unity among Blacks aimed at improving conditions for all Blacks should be encouraged; African America continues to be oppressed by white America, and this oppression has always been the reason for most Black poverty and vice; Black Americans retain and celebrate an African heritage; white supremacy is bad; corporate and financial profiteering continues to divide and impoverish the working class; cultural and racial differentiation is acknowledged and accepted. Therefore, non-Europeans need not assimilate European racial or cultural norms to be co-equal within American pluralism.

Reginald Hudlin, a graduate of Harvard University's film program who is sometimes called the "intellectual gremlin of black independent cinema," makes the point: "For a whole year [after its release] I was asked, 'You're a black filmmaker: What do you think about *The Color Purple?*' And I'd say, 'I think you ought to go see a black independent film: That's what's happening."[21] The Hudlin brothers are among a growing number of young Black and non-Black filmmakers who refuse the Hollywood approach to film production.

THE BLACK FILMMAKER FOUNDATION

By the late 1970s, Black film distributors TAM and Cinemethics International were dead. Over the next decade, Third World Cinema, Women Make Movies, and other nonprofit organizations began to distribute noncommercial and art films by people of color, but their focus was significantly more independent than Hollywood oriented.

In 1978, Warrington Hudlin, a 1974 graduate of Yale University, co-founded and became president of the Black Filmmaker Foundation (BFF), an incorporated, nonprofit arts organization headquartered in New York City. Warrington Hudlin's film career began with his documentary *Black at Yale* (1974) and his undergraduate thesis project, *Street Corner Stories* (1977), a cinema verité piece on the Black community in New Haven, Connecticut. BFF's original mission was to distribute films made by African Americans to libraries, museums, and colleges and to create a dialogue between Black filmmakers and their audience by showing films at community centers and on community access cable channels. By the mid-1980s, it also served as fiscal agent and was commissioned to administer funds awarded to Black filmmakers by other nonprofit organizations. Author and filmmaker Trey Ellis says that BFF is "one of the first black-arts organizations that couples the creativity of the new black artists themselves with the insider's knowledge of high finance from the current flood of young black investment bankers and lawyers."[22] In fact, Black graduates of both Harvard and Yale law schools and Blacks employed on the business side of corporations such as Home Box Office have been BFF board members since the group's inception. Ellis says that BFF's relationship with these professionals is probably what has made it last so long.

Warrington Hudlin became an outspoken critic of Hollywood's continued reluctance to hire African Americans either as actors or behind the camera. He championed the independent spirit exemplified by Melvin Van Peebles's release of *Sweetback*. BFF became a major influence for aspiring filmmakers, such as Spike Lee, whose grants the organization administered. Warrington and other BFF officers became well-known spokespersons before the media and funding sources, as well as at conferences and film festivals where African American or third world filmmaking was concerned.

Spike Lee's NYU student films were also distributed by BFF. Lee gave talks, showed his films, and participated in panel discussions set up by Warrington and the BFF staff. In fact, BFF members, including Reginald Hudlin, appear in Lee's first feature, *She's Gotta Have It* (1986), and helped him mount the production. Proceeds from the New York premiere were donated, at least in part, to BFF. This film's box office success made it the model for other African American filmmakers and for white film financiers and distributors.

ISLAND PICTURES AND *SHE'S GOTTA HAVE IT*

Lee used "creative financing" to produce *She's Gotta Have It* on a low budget of $175,000, and the independent distributor Island Pictures opened the film in a few theaters nationwide. This film tells the story of Nola Darling, who is romantically involved with three very different men who openly resent one another. Jamie is matter-of-fact and appears steadfast. Greer drives a fancy car, knows he's good looking, and cannot understand why Nola doesn't settle down with him alone. Mars is a wisecracking, bicycle-riding, gold-necklace-wearing, unemployed homeboy who keeps Nola laughing. Russell Schwartz, then president of Island Pictures, released *She's Gotta Have It* as a comedy/art feature in 1986, and this affected the American film scene like few art releases before or since.

Though written, produced, and directed by African Americans, *She's Gotta Have It* had its initial critical success at the San Francisco Film Festival, where it played before an audience that was more than 90 percent white. Success in this venue was a primary determining factor in Island's picking up the film and in the structure of its release pattern. Although impressed by Lee's vigorous promotion of a Black middle-class audience hungry for a feature depicting their own race/class image, even before meeting with Lee, Island executives had "a hunch that there was a segment of America that was not being catered to in terms of movies, and we identified that as a Black middle class that we felt was out there . . . And after speaking with [Spike] about it we said that this makes a lot of sense."[23] Releasing this film downtown demonstrated a successful attempt to bring distribution of Black films in line with a new and untested American attitude toward race relations:

> The whole idea was to find and test the limits of a black audience—and to expose them, for the first time in many years at that point—to a film that spoke about relationships, and not one that was standard blaxploitation. . . . Further the reason the film was opened in the Lincoln Center area was to avoid the film being "ghettoized." This was done in full consultation with Spike Lee. The surprise was not that Blacks came, but that WHITES came. Based on this successful opening, we were able to give the film a more commercial playoff throughout Manhattan (including Harlem) and the rest of the country. In effect, *She's Gotta Have It* was a break-through film because it not only attracted a black middle class audience, but a white one as well. If we had opened the film in Harlem initially, we would never have gotten it to cross over.[24]

Although Island was a young company in the mid-1980s, it was a profitable corporation and had built a reputation distributing a number of well-received art films. Statistics and demographics, however, are not the tools relied on by successful distributors. Dennis Greene, former vice president for production at Columbia Pictures, says that "motion pictures are not made on the basis of audience. They're made on the basis of who you want to be in business with."[25] What stars or directors seem to be up-and-coming is more important to a financing company than what statistics say an audience is likely to pay for. This recalls the statement that numbers had nothing to do with Island's decision to distribute *She's Gotta Have It*. In fact, the decision was based on Island's people having seen the film, Lee's conviction that the film would make it, and a "hunch" that the movie would exhibit "legs," or be able to stand on its own.

NEW LINE CINEMA AND *HOUSE PARTY*

Starting with a budget of $3,000, Robert Shay, son of a grocer, created New Line Cinema and distributed foreign films to college audiences in the mid-1970s. In the early 1980s, he bought the expired copyright for a 1940s-era government production aimed at young people and designed to discourage their use of marijuana. For late-1980s youth this film, *Reefer Madness*, was a tremendous, unintentionally comedic success, and its distribution was so profitable that Shay expanded beyond the campus into movie houses.

Real success began for Shay with the production and distribution of the horror-film-genre *Nightmare on Elm Street*, then the *Friday the 13th* series. The audience for these films included college-age youth but extended New Line's reach to younger audiences who were even more dedicated moviegoers. These films developed a cult following sufficient to sustain many profitable sequels. Emerging film companies like New Line stick to producing films in a limited number of genres, that is, films with particular, predetermined or formulaic attributes and elements demonstrated to have appeal for a certain audience segment. New Line both financed and released the Hudlin brothers' first feature film, *House Party*, in 1990 as one in a series of rap music comedies.

The Hudlin brothers' financial success with *House Party* was, in large part, the product of close attention paid to the economic structural developments in the U.S. feature film industry. As they worked for ten years distributing Black independent films through the Black Filmmaker Foundation, they studied the distribution and marketing aspects of the business. Warrington Hudlin, intimately aware of the difficulties Lee encountered in producing the "no-budget" *She's Gotta Have It*, used this knowledge to advantage in negotiations with potential financiers.

Recommended by Lee to film financiers and distributors after his film's success, the Hudlin brothers got their *House Party* produced by independent distributor New Line Cinema for $2.5 million. In March 1990, the film opened in five hundred theaters nationwide with a television, print, and newspaper advertising budget of about $4 million. *House Party*, a feature-length version of a short film Reginald had made as an undergraduate at Harvard, grossed over $30 million in its first six months. It was perhaps the first Black independent feature to attempt to make use of the saturation release and advertising techniques developed by Peter Guber as part of the blockbuster marketing approach. As a result, Warrington Hudlin says, the film grossed more than any other film by a first-time Black feature director and more than any other Black independent film except Spike Lee's *Do the Right Thing* through 1991. The result of this success was quick action on the part of the entertainment industry. The June 27, 1990, issue of *Variety* reported Hudlin brothers contracts with both Tri-Star Pictures and NBC television for multiple productions over the next two or three years.[26]

KJM3: A BLACK FILM DISTRIBUTOR

African Americans, as an audience for feature films, are variously defined and delimited. Jacqueline Bobo reported at the 1992 "Available Visions" film and video conference that in 1988 Blacks spent $1.1 billion on theatrical films. This constituted about one-fourth of $4.5 billion spent nationally.[27] Spike Lee saw *She's Gotta Have It* as marketable to a Black middle-class audience. Island Pictures opened it near Lincoln Center to boost its crossover potential. In order to avoid competition with the majors in the current period, many small companies avoid the inner-city or underclass audience to whom, they say, the majors are addressing their Black films. For example, KJM3, which was the marketing company for Julie Dash's *Daughters of the Dust* and has now become a film distributor, believes that trying to market to the Black urban underclass would put them in direct competition with the majors.[28] KJM3 does not expect to cater to the Black middle class either, because they choose to market films which they call "authentically Black."[29] Professor of African American studies Talmadge Anderson says, "Black arts and literary works are truly authentic when they reflect the condition and experience of African Americans in relation to the broader society and world."[30] KJM3 defines a Black film as one in which all three positions of authority (screenwriter, director, and producer) are held by Blacks and the story content presents a "representation of how Black people interact" that is believable to the general African American audience.[31] Michelle Materre, vice president of KJM3, says that "African American media is that which is produced by African American film and videomakers, rather than that which is produced by others about African Americans."[32] Thus, for KJM3, the cultural circumstances within which characters interact are important and must ring true for Black viewers.[33] Such films are not expected to cross over to a white, general audience.

> KJM3's commitment to the Black audience is a cultural imperative. Our specialized focus on the needs and tastes of the Black audience as a whole puts us in a position to satisfy its entertainment needs. The general market competitors, and the specialized "art house" distributors, are very skilled at targeting the general and specialty markets. However, their traditional approach to reaching out to the Black audience results in those films which reflect the African and African-American experience never achieving their potential performance levels, and an audience hunger that remains unsatisfied. . . . Our releases will be marketed on a market-by-market basis, utilizing a strategy which cross-references the tastes, habits and opinions of the African and African-American viewing audience in order to reach the broadest potential market.[34]

Julie Dash provided the chance to demonstrate the validity of this view by bringing KJM3 and Kino International, distributors of *Daughters of the Dust*, together. Dash's lyric storytelling shows how an extended family of Geechees, Blacks descended from Africans who largely remained on the sea islands off the coast of South Carolina after slavery, decided to migrate north. In their local Gullah dialect of mixed English and African languages, generations of Black women powerfully narrate, debate, and act out their forceful, emotional, and

(*Left to right*) KJM3 vice presidents Mark Walton, Katheryn Bowser, Martin L. Adams, and Michelle A. Materre *(Mel Wright, Photo "95")*

secret responses to years of rape and other oppressions by local whites. Two hallmarks of *Daughters* are a clear, celebrated memory link between enslaved Africans and post-slavery Blacks and presentation of both familial and romantic love between young and old, male and female.

KJM3 marketed *Daughters* to a core audience via their "surgical marketing model," a method of cross-referencing tastes, habits, and entertainment consumption patterns of that core audience. A major component of this model is a profile of an identifiable, targetable market segment called the cultural grassroots.[35] Persons who fit this category may be in the economic underclass, the middle class, or even the small Black upper class. They may be well educated or have little formal training. They may learn African dance or wear traditional African attire and have a strong image of themselves as African. This target group comprises a comparatively small audience and for this reason may have not been respected by general product and media distributors. Yet, in New York and other major American cities, this audience numbers in the millions, and while many of the cultural grassroots will not attend a film for years at a time, they will stand on line for hours to see a film they have heard delivers a representation of African American culture likely to make them feel comfortable. KJM3 used both traditional and nontraditional marketing techniques not only in New York but in New Jersey and Connecticut to promote the film to the cultural grassroots. It arranged interviews on Black radio and television programs, placed stories in major Black mainstream and arts newspapers and magazines, and enlisted the support of many Black social and political organizations. Materre noted that "KJM3 was able to promote *Daughters of the Dust* to Black churches because they contacted the ministers one on one and had them talk it up to their congregations."[36]

Several advance word-of-mouth screenings were held for influential Black people from diverse backgrounds. In addition, KJM3 distributed leaflets describing the film at a variety of venues—at New York–area Black professional organization events normally held during the Kwanzaa-Christmas holiday season, such as the annual Black Expo and the Malcolm X Cultural Conference, both held in New York City, and other events likely to attract Blacks interested in the cultural and political history of Africa and African America. The opening of *Daughters* was scheduled for January 15 to coincide with the nationwide celebration of the Rev. Dr. Martin Luther King Jr.'s legacy and to precede February's annual nationwide celebration of Black history.

KJM3 executives say that they employed this marketing strategy because *Daughters of the Dust* was conceived and funded as a noncommercial, independent work. Materre defines an independent work as one that is "produced primarily as a result of the vision of its director or producer [and] is usually funded 'catch as catch can.'"[37] Hollywood has released so few films that carry cultural and sociopolitical content derived from the lived experiences of diasporic Blacks in Africa, Europe, and the Americas that it has no method for reaching the core audience for *Daughters. Daughters of the Dust* presents such experiences, and white-American-controlled major and "mini-major" distribution companies have not proved competent to reach an audience for them. One might say that a diasporic African work of this type eschews negative stereotyping of

Blacks and is opposed to both implicit and explicit inferences of non-Black and Eurocentric domination in any guise. Such works, even as comedies, are likely to support community, communal defense and development among Black people in any part of the world.

Although KJM3 handled marketing for *Daughters of the Dust*, its premiere distribution effort was with the film *Neria* (1992) by Zimbabwe-born director Godwin Mawuru, which opened at the Biograph Theater in Washington, D.C., in early April. The film follows Neria's fight to hold her family together in the face of traditional cultural customs and rituals of inheritance. It is a modern Zimbabwean story, which the distributor's literature quotes *Variety* as saying "looms as an unusual attraction for African American audience tired of Hollywood exploitation . . . heartwarming." In April and May *Neria* played to sellout crowds at the Lincoln Center's "Modern Days, Ancient Nights: Thirty Years of African Filmmaking" festival in New York City. Another culturally authentic film, *Neria* was promoted using the same marketing strategy that KJM3 used to promote *Daughters*: events attended by the core audience were initially targeted, and word-of-mouth advertising spread interest in the film.

Crossover: Content and Marketing Structure Conflict

Eddie Murphy, one of America's most successful screen personalities, enlisted the Hudlin brothers directing/production team for his film *Boomerang*, to be distributed by Paramount, a major studio. Given the tremendous success of Murphy releases such as *48 Hours* and *Beverly Hills Cop I* and *II*, *Boomerang* received perhaps the largest budget, just under $50 million, of any Black production in history. Although the initial *Boomerang* screenplay was written by whites to attract Murphy's normal audience, Reginald Hudlin altered the film to such an extent that the story became more accessible to Blacks than to whites. The result was that Blacks turned out for the film in large numbers while whites were significantly less inclined to see it. *Los Angeles Times* film reviewer Kenneth Turan, for example, said:

You can tell a performer is in trouble when his legal entanglements are more entertaining than his movies. . . . Watching Murphy in "Boomerang" it is almost impossible to remember the sharp, high-spirited exhilaration he brought to comedy in films like "48 HRS" and "Trading Places." . . . [T]he character he plays . . . is no hustler, no scrambler after respectability, he is a polished and successful director of marketing for a successful cosmetics corporation. . . . Watching the best wisenheimer in the business determinedly turning himself into a sensitive, New Age guy is an exercise in sheer frustration.[38]

In *Hollywood and the Box Office*, John Izod says that a film must make two and a half times its production costs before it breaks even.[39] Grossing $70 million on a production budget of about $50 million, *Boomerang* is considered a domestic financial failure despite excellent reception in the African American community. *Boomerang* turned out not to be a crossover film. However, the final word on this is yet unspoken.[40]

This case provides evidence that culture has box office significance. It also demonstrates that there may be an upper limit on the size of the return that can be expected from a particular market segment. This has implications for how big a film production budget a market segment can support. In contrast to Dennis Greene and Island executives, KJM3 feels that if it is targeting the Black audience with an "authentically Black" product, it may be unwise to finance a higher budget than that audience can profitably reimburse.

Although on a creative plane screenwriters abhor the thought that audience and financial considerations determine their scripts, distributors and investors are naturally very concerned with who is likely to pay to see their releases. It is therefore the business side of filmmaking that tries to match a script with a profitable viewing audience. A major consideration in this regard is how accessible the film will be to a large white audience approaching two hundred million persons, with potential single-film revenues (at an average four dollars per ticket in 1992) of $800 million, as opposed to a smaller Black audience that may number well under ten million with corresponding single-film potential revenues of $40 million. Thus, even before a production budget can be validly considered, the issue of crossover potential must be addressed.

In today's film industry, *crossover* refers to the potential of a film addressing nonwhite Americans' concerns to secure a significant financial return from white American viewers. While one might argue that a film addressing white concerns can conceptually cross over to a nonwhite audience as well, since the real issue is the film's "legs" or moneymaking ability, the size of the white market can *alone* provide very strong legs, so crossover to nonwhites need not be considered seriously. Culture and finance are intimately interwoven within the crossover concept, and because whites control film financing, nonwhite filmmakers must consider their films' crossover potential to attract white private financing.

Yet, Spike Lee says to nonwhite filmmakers, "No, you don't have to cross over. Not at all. That depends on what the film is. There's no law. Like *School Daze*, I knew going in it was gonna be very hard for a white audience to relate to what happens on a Black college campus. Whereas *She's Gotta Have It* was more accessible to them. Same thing with *Do the Right Thing*." But when asked why *She's Gotta Have It*, if it was so accessible to whites, was advertised as a comedy even though he had never viewed it as such, Lee said, "Anytime when there's Black people involved they put 'comedy' on it. Makes it more palatable for the white audiences. Whereas drama, they might be uneasy, might be uneven."[41] Whether or not there is truth in this statement, it indicates that African America's number one filmmaker feels the need to fight industry stereotypes even before his films are written. Films such as *Boyz N the Hood* and *Menace II Society* are condemned for catering to the Blacks-as-violent or criminal stereotypes like those dominant in the blaxploitation period. By contrast, movies featuring Blacks as neither violent nor comic, such as *Daughters of the Dust* and *To Sleep with Anger*, have been very poorly received in distribution circles.

Black films must be presented to white distributors in particular ways that are consistent with white audience stereotyping of Blacks in order to predict crossover success. Such predictions, of course, sometimes go awry. Despite the presence of Eddie Murphy, the crossover champion, for example, many observers believe that because he was in a Black business situation (similar to the Black college situation of *School Daze*), with 90 percent Black characters

Charles Burnett directs Danny Glover in *To Sleep with Anger*
(Museum of Modern Art/Film Stills Archive)

presented as successful professionals, white audiences found *Boomerang* inaccessible, which made it a crossover failure. Turan, for example, found that

> the most intriguing aspect of *Boomerang* turn[ed] out to be not its story but its racial composition. . . . [T]his kind of cinematic affirmative action can be seen as very long overdue, but unlike the dramatically motivated all-black cast of *A Rage in Harlem* [a gangster film in which Blacks mutilate each other] it feels in its own way as silly and arbitrary as mainstream movies without any people of color on screen.[42]

White audiences find Murphy accessible only when he is among 90 percent white characters in a story line aimed specifically at whites culturally. Such films' crossover revenues from a Black audience are a mere bonus since Black cultural considerations are addressed only tangentially, if at all.

Warner Bros.' 1992 release of Spike Lee's film *Malcolm X* is a case in point. When Lee demanded $35 million from Warner Bros. to produce the film he said it deserved the same budget the studio had provided for Oliver Stone's *JFK*. Warner Bros. thought otherwise on the basis that JFK as icon had a much larger potential audience than did Malcolm X. To paraphrase the famous Lloyd Bentsen quip, they were saying, "Spike, your Malcolm is no Kennedy."

That Lee thought his film could command as large an audience as *JFK* reveals how much Malcolm X's image has changed over the years, or at least the kind of image Lee was willing to fashion. Historically, JFK and Malcolm occupied entirely different political spheres. It's hard to imagine any circumstance in which Malcolm would have been invited to tea at Camelot. Nor can we visualize Kennedy, rather than Martin Luther King Jr., smiling and shaking hands with Malcolm in that famous photograph *Do the Right Thing*'s Smiley lugged about. It's also doubtful that Malcolm would have issued a "chickens coming home to roost" statement had King rather than Kennedy been assassinated in 1963. Martin and Malcolm did not agree on strategies and goals, but they were not asymmetrical in the way Malcolm and JFK were. Malcolm and JFK had followings that differed radically in their racial composition, their long-range goals, and, most important, in numbers of persons. Something profound must have happened to the image of Malcolm and/or of JFK over the decades if, in the 1990s, they were considered, by the commercial film industry, capable of attracting equivalent, much less the same, moviegoing audiences. Or perhaps it is the image of Malcolm as shaped by Lee that became compatible with the image of JFK as shaped by Stone.

The major consideration for Warner Bros. regarding *Malcolm X* was whether or not it could get a crossover audience. How else could a $35 million, three-hour-plus epic bring in the nearly $90 million needed to make it a success? Malcolm had been despised by the vast majority of whites during his lifetime and disliked by a majority of Black Americans as well. JFK, in contrast, had a reasonable chance for reelection, and his death transformed him into a national martyr on the scale of President Lincoln. The conspiracy angle to *JFK* added additional dramatic dimensions that seemed lacking in the conventional version of Malcolm's assassination. Put more simply, if one assumes an average national admission price of four dollars, and if 50 percent of all thirty million African Americans bought a ticket to see *Malcolm X*, the box office return would be $60

Angela Bassett and Denzel Washington in *Malcolm X*
(Cineaste/David Lee)

million. If 50 percent of the two hundred million white Americans bought tickets, the return would be $400 million. This nearly seven-fold gap in returns determined Warner Bros.' consideration that a crossover audience, and not a Black audience alone, had to be the primary market for *Malcolm X.*

To meet that need, Lee dampened every controversial aspect of Malcolm's life as well as many of the period's specifically Black cultural referents. Malcolm, for instance, is the only Black person in the film to use the term "Daddy-O." This exemplifies the dilemma faced by any African American filmmaker who wants to attract mass, or crossover, market dollars. When he or she views white filmmakers and their works as the primary models, the tolerance level and cultural biases of the white audience become critical.

Unlike Warner Bros., however, KJM3 is not in the crossover business. It expects to get 100 percent of its revenues from the cultural grassroots, a segment of the Black audience numbering probably well under five million with a potential single-film revenue of $20 million maximum. Dividing this maximum revenue by the break-even ratio of 2.5 equals a maximum production cost per film of $8.8 million. Applying this same reasoning, with a budget of $50 million, projected revenues for *Boomerang* must have been $125 million. Yet, from an admittedly high ten-million-person potential Black audience, only a maximum of $40 million could be expected. Paramount must have expected the other $85 million to come from the white community. It did not. In fact, total first-year domestic receipts were $15 million short of the $85 million whites must have been projected to provide and double that expected from Blacks. At a cost of $800,000, by contrast, and revenues of $1.8 million in thirty-three rather than fifty-two weeks, with an audience that was perhaps 90 percent Black, *Daughters of the Dust* exceeded expectations.

The need to cross over in order to satisfy distribution company demands for box office return impinges on African American filmmakers' ability to depict African America's political life and culture.

Reassertion of the Majors' Dominance over Film Distribution

The majors' neglect of exhibitor needs in the 1970s allowed independent distributors and producers to gain ground. In the mid-1970s, theatrical release of films written, directed, and produced by Blacks was virtually nonexistent. The majors dominated film distribution with high-cost, culturally white blockbusters such as *Star Wars* and *Indiana Jones*. Now, in the early 1990s, by contrast, the success of tiny distribution companies, such as Kino International, has inspired the creation of still smaller, culturally focused companies such as KJM3. But this is by no means the end of the story. While only the majors can afford to experiment with the expense of making blockbusters, they are simultaneously enticing new Black filmmakers the independents have proved successful and buying existing independents and creating new, "boutique" distributors of their own.

The majors have also begun to experiment with hiring young Black filmmakers untested even in the independent arena. The best two examples of this are the Columbia Pictures financing of features by then-twenty-three-year-old John Singleton in 1990 and "twenty-

something" Darnell Martin (she won't tell her age) in 1993. Singleton's film, *Boyz N the Hood*, grossed nearly $60 million on a produc-
tion budget of between $6 and $8 million. Martin's *I Like It Like
That*, which opened in October 1994, cost $5.5 million and grossed
a very disappointing $1.2 million in its first year. It was the first fea-
ture directed by an African American woman with Hollywood financing and distribution.[43]

Spike Lee says that a small distribution company is almost
doomed to failure. Of KJM3 he says, "I don't know how [they're]
gonna do distribution, you gotta have tons of money. First of all anytime you start out, especially if you're Black, the majors, they're
gonna try to crush you."[44] The reality of this threat is brought home
by the fact that Island, which released *She's Gotta Have It* in 1986,
has been forced out of domestic distribution due to severe competition from the majors. Orion, New World, and Vestron Pictures, all
thought to be distribution companies with bright futures in the mid-
1980s, have either filed for bankruptcy or significantly reduced their
distribution activities. Samuel Goldwyn, Inc., which released Robert Townsend's *Hollywood Shuffle*, has not proved to be an aggres-
sive player in the 1990s Black film arena. In fact, since 1990 the
major players in the distribution of Black independent feature film
productions have been the majors themselves. The champion of all
Black independent producers, Spike Lee, is a willing participant in
this reaggregation of U.S. film distribution.

Since the independent Island Pictures released his first film in
1986, Lee has gone from one major to another: first Columbia for
School Daze, Universal for *Do the Right Thing*, *Mo' Better Blues*, and
Jungle Fever, Warner Bros. for *Malcolm X*, and back to Universal for
Crooklyn (1993) and *Clockers* (1995). Of course, it is reasonable that
a talented filmmaker will outgrow a company whose financing abilities are limited, but Island is no longer sponsoring up-and-coming
filmmakers. It is, rather, out of the domestic film business altogether.
Lee has started to play executive producer for films by other filmmakers. He is neither writer, director, nor producer on these new
projects. He merely approves a script and attaches studio production
financing and distribution, as Steven Spielberg did on the *Back to*

the Future series. Lee's first executive production, *The Drop Squad*, opened in October 1994. It was financed and distributed by Universal's new low-budget subsidiary, Gramercy Pictures, of which Russell Schwartz is president. Schwartz, formerly an independent distributor, is now part of the Hollywood establishment.

Like Spike Lee, the Hudlin brothers moved from independent to Hollywood distribution companies. They were with New Line for *House Party*, then a two-film deal with Columbia subsidiary Tri-Star was rumored but never realized, then they went to Paramount for *Boomerang* with Eddie Murphy and for their animated feature *Bebe's Kids*. In 1994, the Hudlin brothers moved their offices from New York City to the 20th Century Fox lot in Los Angeles. Their latest venture was *Cosmic Slop*, a ninety-minute special produced and aired on Home Box Office (HBO), which is part of the Time Warner corporation. *Cosmic Slop* was described in the *New York Times* as something "more than a multicultural 'Twilight Zone,' with a bit of 'Playhouse 90' and 'Yo! MTV Raps!' thrown in."[45]

With the success of *House Party* and *Teenage Mutant Ninja Turtles*, New Line graduated to the category of mini-major and created its own art distribution subsidiary, Fine Line. In 1994, New Line merged with Atlanta-based Turner Communications Company.

Robert Townsend went from Samuel Goldwyn for *Hollywood Shuffle* to 20th Century Fox for *The Five Heartbeats*. Charles Lane went from *Sidewalk Stories* at Goldwyn to Disney, where he was hired to direct *True Identity*.

The majors, then, are not allowing the course of feature film distribution to be taken from their hands. Rather than shun Black filmmakers, they endorse and sponsor them. In this blockbuster period, the majors may be using generally low-budget Black film productions to pad the package offered exhibitors. Traditionally "B" and genre films were used as padding. Low-budget films by African Americans, however, provide the added bonus of addressing racial inclusion complaints voiced by the NAACP and still serve the purpose of keeping the majors' competition at bay.

In a sense, Black filmmakers may be seen as pawns manipulated in white distributors' power games. While this may, in fact, be the case, the question from many African American filmmakers' point of view is really to what extent can they manipulate the distributors to continue getting their productions seen and to gain more influence in the industry. At one time, Warrington Hudlin said that Black filmmakers were the exploited cheap laborers of the industry because their productions were financed at such a low level but gained such a high relative return. But the Hudlin brothers' film *Boomerang* had a higher budget than a great number of white filmmakers have been allowed. Though it was less profitable at the box office than had been expected, this does not appear to have harmed the brothers' outlook for future production financing. In addition to the yet-to-be-realized two-picture Tri-Star deal, the Hudlins still have television offers and are in the early stages of executive producing other filmmakers' productions. Robert Townsend, whose *Five Heartbeats* also bombed despite continued good reviews from individual African American viewers, has completed his third feature, *Meteor Man*. For Gramercy, Mario Van Peebles directed *Posse*, the first Black western since the 1972 *Buck and the Preacher*. Independent distributor Miramax, now teamed with Disney, released the second feature by an African American woman, the low-budget *Just Another Girl on the IRT*. In fact, those "in the mix" generally feel that if you're Black and not getting money out of Hollywood now, something's seriously wrong with you. And, unlike the blaxploitation period of the 1970s, Black people are *behind* and *in front* of the camera now. This means that Blacks have significant decision-making authority once a studio has decided to work with a picture. True, corporate board rooms and executive suites remain largely white and male, but the Spike Lee phenomenon has allowed a few Blacks a new level of entree into the film industry.

Although there are reasons for optimism, however, it is important to remember that Hollywood's openness to African Americans is the result of a structural aberration. It is much too early to call this the norm. The majors may find new ways to make larger profits without Blacks, as happened in the beginning of the blockbuster period. The independent distributors who introduced most of the new Black filmmakers have largely joined the Hollywood establishment.

The resulting structural environment, where the majors own boutique distributors and are expanding their control of cable and theatrical distribution venues, is too tight to predict success for a new crop of independents. African American filmmakers who have distribution deals are likely to support this trend because it brings a higher level of professionalism to their projects.

Chapter 6 Employment Discrimination

Despite the prospects offered by new communications technologies, African Americans continue to encounter racism in the film industry. At 1969 Equal Employment Opportunity Commission hearings in Los Angeles on minority employment in the movie industry, one studio official testified that of eighty-one people in management only three were minorities: two Latinos, one Black. The Black headed the janitorial department. Of 184 technicians five were minorities: three Latinos, one Black, one Asian. At this time, minorities comprised 40 percent of the Los Angeles metropolitan area population but only 3 percent of the movie industry labor force.[1]

In a 1977 U.S. Commission on Civil Rights investigation of television, a TV union was revealed to have had a scheme to phase out Blacks who attained union membership by "seeking their suspension without due process hearings."[2] The commission's inquiry revealed that the investigation of the movie industry eight years earlier had had no significant effect on hiring practices in the Los Angeles–based television industry. The commission concluded it was unlikely that any minority culture was accurately televised during the three years from 1974 to 1976, since "not even one minority person obtained work . . . as either a script supervisor or a story analyst" in this period.[3]

Litigation by unions such as the Directors Guild of America (DGA), the Screen Actors Guild (SAG), and the Writers Guild of America (WGA) and, most important, a threat to both litigate and boycott the majors' films by the NAACP were major tactics employed to increase racial minority presence in the feature film industry. In mid-1980, Chester L. Migden, chief negotiator for SAG, whose members include the biggest names in Hollywood, stated that only one major studio, 20th Century Fox, had been forthcoming on the issue of affirmative action under the old agreement with the union. SAG was then pushing the majors for contractual assurance of compliance under new contracts soon to be negotiated. "This time," Migden declared, "there can be no avoiding the responsibility to create a meaningful affirmative action program."[4]

Black independent filmmaker Oliver Franklin delineated two schools of thought on how to increase minority representation in the industry: (1) the Booker T. Washington approach where minorities would "make their own films" or (2) getting more minorities into Hollywood.[5] In January 1982, the NAACP had already embarked on the second course with a vengeance. *Variety*, the bible of the working film industry, reported an agreement between executives from three major studios and Motion Picture Academy president Jack Valenti, on one side, and Benjamin Hooks, former commissioner of the Federal Communications Commission and then president of the NAACP, on the other, to put off until February 1 a threatened NAACP-sponsored, nationwide boycott of new films released by the majors. By that date the majors were to "supply specific information on minority employment practices," to be compared with the NAACP's own records. The stated goal of these meetings was to establish "a concrete program designed to remove employment inequities" in the feature film and television industries.[6] The NAACP considered its boycott threat credible because its research showed that Blacks comprised 30 percent of America's moviegoing audience. Hooks stated that "the 1800 NAACP branches will not only head a campaign to discourage Black patronage but will bus its followers and members to 'lily white neighborhoods' if needed."[7]

In February, however, Hooks found the majors' statistics "too general in classification." Valenti refused to give "individual studio-by-studio figures on the hiring of Blacks and other minorities," saying, "If the objective is to see how employment is doing, then the consolidated figures [of all the majors combined] are what they need." Valenti further suggested that he had already "outlined his ongoing plans to improve industry minority hiring practices" and that the NAACP might "review his progress in a year." Hooks complained that the majors "did not supply specific job descriptions, and gave only an overview." The NAACP needed "individual studio statistics" to avoid punishing "innocent companies" in a boycott.[8]

By August, the NAACP had decided to boycott the single major studio expected to be "most vulnerable" to direct action rather than the one found to be "most discriminatory," and it established the Port Gibson Direct Action Institute of California to "train black leaders in the art of selective patronage."[9] Collet Wood, executive director of the Hollywood NAACP chapter, said in a radio call-in that many besides NAACP members had agreed to support a boycott. "Underneath the tip of this iceberg is a mountain of others suffering from the same problem. Orientals. Chicanos. White producers and writers who have tried to get studios to do Black material and were told that the studios didn't want to do those projects."[10]

In the closing months of 1982, Los Angeles city government agencies examined the issue of minority employment in the film and television industry. In September, the Los Angeles Human Relations Commission held three days of hearings on the subject. Called to appear before the commission were the Hollywood unions, associations, and guilds; advertising agencies and advertising representatives for companies such as General Foods and Colgate; the NBC, ABC, and CBS television networks; large independent film production companies; large television production companies such as Spelling, Goldberg, and Lorimar; and all eight of the major studios, plus Disney. An important outcome of these hearings was the commission's request that the Los Angeles City Council "amend the City ordinance regarding acquisition of film permits, which would require film or tv companies requesting access to facilities owned by the public to have some form of an affirmative action plan in regards to the hiring of minorities."[11]

Variety itself seemed to be pressuring the film industry to open to minorities. Its front-page headline on December 1 read, in huge thick print, "Black Pic Employment Still Lags." In this article *Variety* observed that rather than deal with the problem of minority employment, the industry tried to go around it. Of the eight films with Black leading roles released by the majors in 1982, Richard Pryor, a proven box office draw, was in three. "The state of black employment in U.S. feature films has not improved . . . and behind the camera opportunities for black filmmakers have dried up."[12]

Dried up? Was *Variety* saying that there had been more opportunity for Blacks in the past? Yes. In an accompanying article in the same issue entitled "Black Pic Outlook Dark," *Variety* observed that ten years earlier, in 1972, thirty-nine pictures starring Blacks were released and that 1973 saw forty-five released as "black oriented feature films, dozens of which were released by the major distributors, dominated *Variety*'s Top Grossers." *Variety* reported that in the early 1980s, Blacks were not even getting their traditional exploitative or stereotypical roles. "A sign of the times domestically is that one of the most successful exploitation films of 1982, Billy Fine's *The Concrete Jungle*, featured no blacks in key roles. The mandatory ethnic variety of the women's prison format was covered instead by casting Latina types . . . in parts Pam Grier and Brenda Sykes would probably have filled a decade back." In horror films, *Variety* continued, "where blacks account for a dominant portion of ticket sales . . . few on-screen roles for blacks are in evidence."[13]

Through 1983, the industry guilds and the majors were in constant struggle on the issue of affirmative action. While Disney and MGM/UA signed agreements with the NAACP to expand Black participation both in-house "and throughout the motion picture industry," the other five majors declined to so do.[14] In April, a *Variety* article headlined "Break Down of H'wood Minority Hiring" detailed a "wide range of minority underemployment" and quoted the "Screen Actors Guild Minority Report," an accounting based on a 1980 SAG contract, "which required each studio to supply the union with detailed quarterly reports on minority casting."[15] The headline for an accompanying article read "Casting Report by SAG Shows Minorities Lose" and noted that during 1982 312 whites in Hollywood earned over $50,000. Eighty-two of these whites earned over $100,000. Only seven Hispanics and ten Blacks earned over $50,000, and only nineteen Hispanics earned over $25,000, compared to 931 whites. Of the one thousand actors nominated for the Academy Award in the organization's fifty-five-year history, only eight had been Black.[16] This data demonstrated the tremendous income disparity between major American racial groups within the same labor union and led *Variety* to imply possible racial bias on the part of major producing and distributing organizations in favor of hiring whites more frequently and for more lucrative roles.

In mid-1983, the Directors Guild of America received from the federal Equal Employment Opportunity Commission "the nod to file a Class-Action Discrimination suit against . . . the three networks, the major film studios and several large independent producers."[17] A recent one-year DGA study had found that out of 237 directors, Columbia had hired only one minority; Fox two of 146; Universal nineteen of 779; Warner Bros. one of 147; none at Paramount, MGM/ UA, or Disney. While minorities and women made up about 9 percent of DGA members, *Variety* observed, "for the last three quarters [they] have done less than 5 percent of all the work handled by guild members in all categories." What the DGA wanted from the suit was something SAG had recently refused to seek from the industry: that "flexible minimum hiring levels [and] a timeframe within which to reach those goals . . . be a part of any eventual understanding."[18] J. D. Hall and Doris Weaver, members of SAG's board of directors, had resigned from the guild's Hollywood Committee on Wages and Working Conditions when it refused to make "numerical goals" for minority hiring part of SAG's bargaining package.[19] DGA suits against Warner Bros. and Columbia Pictures accused each of violating Title VII of the Civil Rights Act of 1964 in no uncertain terms. Warner was said to

> 'intentionally' deny women and minority DGA members their right to equal employment opportunities. . . . W[arner] B[ros.] officials responsible for making hiring and assignment decisions are 'virtually all white and all-white all-male [and] engage in nepotistic practices, preferring their male and white friends. . . . [Warner Bros.'] 'word of mouth' recruiting system [in which women and minorities] tend not to be notified of or considered for job openings . . . results in the hiring of 'less qualified' whites and males over the hiring of 'more qualified' women and minorities. . . . [O]fficials engage in conscious and unconscious race and sex stereotyping, thereby excluding women and minorities from employment.[20]

Columbia Pictures was said to subject women and minorities to an "illegal discriminatory employment system" since they had been refused jobs due to race or sex and/or "discouraged from seeking employment due to Columbia's reputation for discriminating against racial minorities and women." Columbia's hiring authorities were said to have "no standards, requirements or guidelines" for hiring, and "virtually all of the persons who carry out this totally subjective employment system are men and are members of the white race."[21] *Variety* expressed dismay particularly at Columbia's refusal to accept goals and timetables in light of the fact that its parent company, Coca-Cola, and Operation PUSH had agreed to a goal of 12.5 percent Black managers by 1986.[22] Both Warner Bros. and Columbia filed countersuits against the DGA. Columbia, in its own defense, stated that "its conduct in the past has been non-discriminatory, lawful and proper." DGA pointed out that in the first nine months of 1983, 97 percent of Columbia's directors' jobs went to white males. Of the forty-five first-time TV and film director work days available, all went to white males.[23]

While one may argue that minorities seeking industry employment lack requisite skills, this cannot be said of minority group members already in the industry craft unions. Every person in these organizations has passed professional, day-to-day, on-the-job, and, in some cases, written examinations that attest to member qualification. In fact, even SAG admitted that there were few minorities in its union because "a form of de facto discrimination is at work." It required either past motion picture or TV experience or a producer's promise of it for membership, and it was difficult for minorities to get either.[24]

Variety reported on a 1987 WGA employment study of 5,434 writers broken down by gender, race, age, number of people hired, and salary differentials. The report showed that "white male scripters have the advantage in every sector of the industry—the majors, independents, networks, smaller companies and in both feature films and tv."[25] Not much had changed since Black writers had discussed "Hollywood's color problem" in an article five years earlier: Pamela Douglas, former vice president at Universal Television, said, "Whites will not hire us to do white scripts—only black ones." But Black writers were employed on only one episode of television's "Black" sensation *Roots*; Bernie Rollins of the WGA Black Writers Committee said, "They told us, 'You are too close to the material; you won't do justice to it.'" According to author Robert Price, "The agents who sell to producers tell us that there is no market for black material . . . the producers tell the public that there are no black writers." And on *Star Trek II*, a white stuntman was painted Black to double for Paul Winfield "even though the Black Stuntmen's Association has seventeen male members."[26]

The fact that professional writers—who have demonstrated the requisite skills by being industry union members—are refused jobs is telling. What can explain white industry operatives' continued refusal to hire even qualified Blacks? Spike Lee asks, "Why does Barbara Streisand do *Yentl*? Everything Woody Allen does is Jewish. Look at Scorsese with Little Italy. How come they can do things with their culture," while Blacks and other colored people are "too close" to do things with theirs?[27] The implication is that for jobs in the U.S. feature film industry, skin color matters. As longtime director Daniel Mann observed with regard to famed cinematographer James Wong Howe some years ago, "What an amazing man to be able to withstand all the pressure, because there are many who look upon Jimmie, not as a man first, but as an Oriental."[28] Chris Hodenfield, editor of *American Film* magazine, has noted:

> There is an exclusive men's club in Los Angeles that has, in its membership, the town's real power brokers—the captains of industry, publishing and banking. Responsible citizens, you'd suppose. Throughout this century, it was custom at this club to make the mayor of Los Angeles an honorary member. In 1973, that custom stopped. No reason was ever given. But that was the year Tom Bradley was first elected mayor. He's a black man.[29]

Lest we think that Hollywood has opened to nonwhites since the 1973 election of Tom Bradley, and that kind of thing is an exception, Joy Horowitz in the March 1989 issue of *Premiere* says otherwise.

> At a time when Hollywood has released the civil-rights film *Mississippi Burning*, at a time when blacks dominate every sphere of American pop culture—from Eddie Murphy at the box office to Bill Cosby on television to Michael Jackson in music—it is a stunning irony that there are no major black executives or agents in the motion picture industry.
>   No one says it out loud, but race is a dirty little secret in

Award-winning director of photography James Wong Howe
(Museum of Modern Art/Film Stills Archive)

> Hollywood power politics. In the movie industry, it's not the
> "L" word, liberal, that people deny. It's the "R" word: racist.[30]

In September 1992, Robert W. Welkos of the *Los Angeles Times* reported the president of the Beverly Hills–Hollywood chapter of the
NAACP as saying that with the exception of two African American
executives at Sony's Columbia Pictures, Inc., "no African Americans
hold creative positions at the level of vice president or above at
Disney, Universal, 20th Century Fox, Metro-Goldwyn-Mayer, Paramount and Warner Bros."[31] What the lack of African American executives means is that no one Black can "green light" a film, that is,
make the decision on behalf of the distribution company to finance
its production. In order for an African American film to get studio
production dollars, then, it must meet the distribution and market-

ing criteria determined by non-Black executives. A 1993 *Wall Street Journal* article quotes African American director Mario Van Peebles on the difficulties thereby engendered:

> After *New Jack City*, I went around pitching another type of story, a black family drama. But they kept wanting to put the family in the 'hood or on crack. "Hey," they'd say, "the movies that make money are killer or shoot-em-up movies. Whatever makes money."[32]

The distribution companies may, however, have a solution to their problem of how to get box office dollars from African America. A major British newspaper reported in 1991 that "with a couple of white-directed 'black' films already rumored to be in the Hollywood pipeline, the possibility of the takeover and exploitation of realistic and sometimes stereotypical images of African-Americans happening again is real."[33] The reason this is not always possible is that it takes time for whites to recognize new African American styles and then learn to copy them such that a new generation of African Americans will pay to see them on screen. *White Men Can't Jump* and *Who's the Man* are but two of a number of feature releases that fit this bill.

Without individual initiative and skill development, racial minorities in America could not hold jobs in the feature film industry. But even in 1990, without group-sponsored litigation very few properly skilled minority group members were able to gain entree. The seeds for expanded African American control behind the camera, however, were laid in this period when the Hollywood distribution and exhibition systems came into conflict.

Chapter 7 Black Women in the System

In stark contrast to the distribution and audience support accorded Black men in the decade since *She's Gotta Have It* ushered in a new distribution era for African American filmmakers, as of March 1995, only about one-tenth of the fifty or so theatrical releases with African American directors had been directed by women. The first of that handful of films did not appear until late 1991, despite calls from New Line, Columbia Pictures, the American Film Institute, and other film industry entities for screenplays and participation in training programs by women of color. Why has the progress of Black filmmakers been so one-sided in terms of gender even as African American women make significant steps in other areas of business and public life?

Black women have been active filmmakers since the blaxploitation period. Julie Dash, for example, was enrolled in the American Film Institute directors' program in the 1970s after having completed the undergraduate film program at City College of New York. Ayoka Chenzira was an early executive director of the Black Filmmaker Foundation in the 1970s and has made a number of animated short films since that time. But as of 1992,

> the Hollywood studio system [had] produced and distributed the work of only one black woman director, the Martinique-born Euzhan Palcy (*A Dry White Season*). Of the 450 features released in 1991 by the studios and major independent companies, 12 were directed by black men and none by black women.[1]

In 1990, New Line Cinema began asking specifically for scripts by and about women of color, what they called "ensemble pieces."

Janet Grillo, New Line's vice president for productions acquisition, said in 1992 that her company "developed a couple but they just didn't come together."[2] New Line actually paid one or more Black women writers and worked with them to develop scripts but decided for one reason or another not to produce the projects. Since 1990, however, New Line has financed and released *House Party, House Party II* and *III, Hangin' with the Homeboys, Deep Cover, Talkin' Dirty after Dark,* and other features written and/or directed by Black men. Aspiring African American woman film director Crystal Emory's script *Sweet Nez* was brought to New Line in 1992 by former Motown Recording Company executive Suzanne dePasse with much fanfare, but New Line passed on it because it was a drama. *Nez* is a "girlz n the 'hood" story in which the heroine returns to school, then becomes a successful entrepreneur after friends' violent deaths teach her that drug dealing does not pay. However, in 1992 New Line released *Deep Cover,* a drama about a Black rookie cop's realization that drug kingpins exalt money over race. About that film, Grillo said:

> The films that New Line is in business to produce are the following: horror movies, comedies for a youth audience and thrillers. Something that we would have liked to have produced but did not was *The Hand That Rocks the Cradle.* [*Deep Cover*] was something that fell between two benches and was kind of a problem for us. It ended up doing well because it was so well made. . . . *Deep Cover* is an urban drama. . . . Our marketing people thought they were getting an action movie. That's a different genre which is a lot easier to sell.

New Line solved this marketing problem by focusing on *Deep Cover*'s action elements and selling it as a genre film rather than a drama. According to Grillo:

> Although *Deep Cover* had aspects that were more of a character drama versus all-action genre, we sold it as an action piece. But those genre elements were there so we could position it in the marketplace versus if it had been exclusively a character drama, which is what *Hangin' with the Homeboys* actually was, and why it failed in release despite film festival awards and great critical reviews and reception.

Director Bill Duke and Jeff Goldblum on the set of *Deep Cover*
(Museum of Modern Art/Film Stills Archive)

One wonders if New Line would have passed on *Boyz N the Hood* since it, like *Sweet Nez*, was also an urban drama. *Nez* was also "less gritty" than *Boyz*, according to Grillo, and therefore less attractive to New Line. New Line's production and release of *Menace II Society* (1993) indicated a change in company policy, Grillo said, since it "was an urban drama, but it had action and gunfire to appeal to a commercial audience." In mid-1993, New Line produced, developed, and released *Who's the Man*, a comedy-action genre film, with Grace Blake, an African American who has held a variety of influential production jobs, working as line producer. This film was written and directed by white men and had a mostly Black male rapper cast. Grillo noted: "One of the film's two producers, Maynell Thomas, was a Black woman. Suzanne dePasse, another Black woman, also executive produced it. The story itself was created by the movie's stars, two Black male comedians, Dr. Dre and Ed Lover. The screenplay was written from that idea by a white man, with the ongoing input of Dre and Ed." While it does not fit the Black Filmmaker Foundation's definition of a Black film, because its director and writer were white, the three African American women

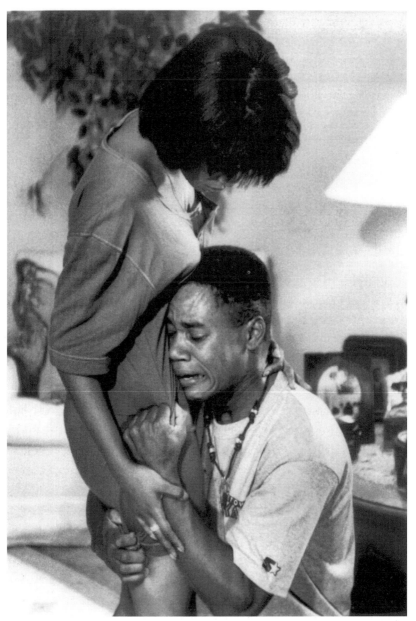

Nia Long and Cuba Gooding Jr. in *Boyz N the Hood* (Cineaste)

producers had tremendous formal and informal influence on subject matter and on hiring decisions.

In late 1992, Grillo pointed out, New Line was developing an "all-gal thing" (female writer, producer, director) called *Getting Lucky* for the Black female rap duo Salt-N-Pepa.

> It's the next place to hit . . . stories from "the sistahs," you know. But you've got to find the right one. It can't be too . . . soft. You know something, this is the issue with women's film, white or Black. . . . It gets down to the same difference between TV movie and theatrical feature movie. There's something in the concept that has to be much more . . . electrifying, uh, genre oriented . . . Commercial! It can't just be a human story about a bunch of gals, you know. It must have a concept, a gimmick, a hook.

The implication is that women of color lose production opportunities due to the subject matter and slant of their stories. Apparently New Line never found the right hook for *Getting Lucky*; by fall 1995 it was in turnaround, meaning that New Line was hoping to sell the project and get back the money already invested. The company was trying to attach casts to and complete the budget for two other films with Black female leads: an action film with four Black women as central characters, written by Black male attorney Takashi Bufford and Kate Lanier (who is white) and to be directed by Gary Gray (also white); and a "rags-to-riches" story about two girls from Brooklyn who are living with a rich, elderly man in Beverly Hills when he suddenly dies.[3]

Grillo outlined two routes for a soft, human development story: either make a low-budget art film or attach a big star, "like Whitney Houston," and do a $15 to $20 million project. In fact, however, with production budgets at around $5 million and with a more-than-ten-year history, New Line has released many pictures that do not meet its genre classifications. *Waterland*, from New Line's subsidiary, Fine Line Features, and *Glengarry Glen Ross*, for example, are neither teen comedy, thriller, nor horror pictures, although both were written and directed by white men. This is where the significance of *independent* production is revealed and interacts with considerations of race and gender. Grillo made a forceful, informative argument against any conclusion that genre categorization applies more strictly to women/minority productions than to those by white males:

> The truth is, either get big stars attached to character dramas, or make character dramas without stars for "no budget"—like Leslie Harris did with *Just Another Girl on the IRT*, and then hope for distribution upon completion. Otherwise, women have to make genre films with mainstream, commercial narrative elements, just like men do—witness Katherine Bigelow, making *Point Break*—to get projects financed by industry sources. You won't help Black women to advance by feeding them paranoid fantasies that special rules apply to them that white men are excused from. There are laws of market value in the commercial film world which apply across the board, across gender or culture. The Hudlins, who are very commercially oriented, understand this as well as anyone. *House Party* was a teen comedy on a low budget, which launched them. Their next picture, *Boomerang*, was a mainstream comedy with a major box office star. They followed the rules of the marketplace, and succeeded in a big way.
>
> If a filmmaker elects to pursue personal, low budget, art film making, then different market rules apply. There will be less money (if any) available from industry sources in getting the films made, because the ultimate audience is smaller. Thus, investment is riskier. Character dramas tend to be personal, sophisticated stories for the smaller, riskier, art house crowd—be they made by men or women. Black or white. This is the larger perspective of the truly independent filmmaker, of which women and Black women can be a subset, if they share these same creative goals, vs having more commercial, mainstream aspirations, as the Hudlins do.
>
> *Waterland* was an art film, which was not produced by New Line, but acquired for distribution when completed, by Fine Line, a subsidiary of New Line, which markets and distributes art films. . . . [T]here is a place for character dramas in our system, as art films of the sort represented by *Waterland*, and released by Fine Line. Also, *Glengarry Glen Ross* was not a New Line production, either. We put up a distribution guarantee to release it in certain markets, but we did not develop or production finance the film. We put up the distribution guarantee because of the A-list of stars involved in the project. This, also, was the other condition I cited by which character dramas fit

into the New Line mandate—if produced with major stars for $15 to $20 million. . . . New Line's involvement with these films in this way has nothing to do with the fact that these two films were made by white men. The two films followed certain rules of marketplace value, that justified New Line or Fine Line's *limited* distribution risk. No production financing or activity was engaged by the corporation in either case.[4]

Gramercy Pictures, a young boutique distribution company headed by former Island Pictures president Russell Schwartz, released its first film, *Posse*, directed by Mario Van Peebles, in 1993. Formed in 1992 as a collaboration between Universal Pictures and Polygram Records, in its first six months of existence Gramercy had one woman—and she was African American—on its A-list of directors for the early 1990s. By 1995, however, Gramercy had yet to release a film by an African American woman. Having even a single Black female director on hand in a film company's first six months is a real change for the better in Hollywood. Not having distributed one of her films after three years smacks of business as usual. One Gramercy executive explained that the lack of female directors simply

> mirrors the whole of American society. How many female executives are high up and how many *Black* female executives are there. Someone has to just commit to making [a film by a woman of color] and there'll be a little golden era of that happening.

A big holdup in producing films by women of color is that 50 percent of all domestic financing comes from overseas. This is what Gramercy's productions are dependent on, despite its attachment to Polygram and Universal. Gramercy's productions are budgeted at $5 to $8 million. Makers of $1 to $2 million movies

> will get those pictures made the same way Spike got *She's Gotta Have It* made. . . . The tenacity of those young directors will be the same whether they're white, Black, Asian, Nuyorican, whatever. When you get into the higher budgets that's where the economics of financing a movie have an impact. There are very few working directors because the financing of movies is so dependent on overseas dollars.[5]

Mario Van Peebles (*center*) directs and stars in *Posse*
(*Cineaste*)

The U.S. market, where the films must prove themselves, has not demonstrated the financial viability of the stories African American women are creating.

Black women do not disagree with the ostensible reasons distributors have given for not supporting their films, but they do find an unspoken rationale as well. Yvonne Welbon notes:

> Together, America's black women filmmakers are creating a small revolution through their style, stories, and strategies. They are forging ahead with or without the blessings of Hollywood, which has conspicuously ignored them in its rush to embrace the newly prominent and profitable crop of black male directors [who make "homeboy" films].[6]

In other words, Black women are consciously, if not deliberately, making films with subject matter outside the norm of Hollywood. The question of Hollywood support for Black women is, then, will a compromise in favor of distribution be reached where Black women alter their subject matter toward the Hollywood norm or will Hollywood begin to support story types currently being voiced by Black female directors?

The words of Julie Dash, writer, producer, and director of *Daughters of the Dust*, the first feature film by an African American woman to receive American theatrical distribution, are instructive. Dash observes that

> when you watch a movie you either role play or disengage. And most white men don't want to be a black woman for two hours. It's two hours too long. But they will spend those same two hours being a homey, because it's a male fantasy and they can walk out of the theater without worry about getting shot.[7]

Daughters of the Dust is a perfect example of what Grillo labels a "soft" film. It would be impossible to call this film gritty. While it seems unlikely that a struggling, independent filmmaker like Dash would have turned down a viable New Line offer, its genre marketing focus might not have made New Line the best distributor for Dash to go with. In addition, the film's production budget of $800,000 was low by New Line standards, and its return of $1.8 million in only thirty-three weeks, while successful, was far below a mini-major's financial expectations. Julie Dash said that she

knew that it would be difficult to get other people to understand the vision of this unusual film. I knew it would be different from the films most people were used to, and there weren't
many people willing to invest in an "untraditional" black
movie. . . . Hollywood studios . . . could not process the fact that
a black woman filmmaker wanted to make a film about African
American women at the turn of the century—particularly a film
with a strong family, with characters who weren't living in the
ghetto, killing each other and burning things down. . . . They
believed that they knew better than we did about what moved
black people.[8]

Despite the nontraditional nature of her film, Julie Dash "just did it."

In 1986, Dash began building finances for her film with grants
from the National Endowment for the Arts, the Fulton County (Georgia) Arts Council, the Georgia Council on the Humanities, and the
Appalshop/Southeast Media Fellowship Program. With these monies, still not enough to shoot her entire film, she produced a sample
and carried it, the completed script, and her filmography, which included a number of prize-winning shorts, to other potential funding
sources in both Europe and the United States. Two of her primary
support organizations at this stage were the National Black Women's
Health Project and Women Make Movies, which raised $5,000 for
her project. In 1988, Dash met Lynn Holst, director of program
development for American Playhouse at the PBS Rocky Mountain
Retreat in Utah. This meeting resulted in American Playhouse providing $650,000, the lion's share of *Daughters*'s $800,000 budget.

In a demonstration of commitment to film that no man could
match, on learning that she was pregnant, Dash decided to have an
abortion rather than put off production of her film for another year.[9]
After the film was completed, she was certain, distribution would
not be a problem. The studios

wouldn't have to imagine a film about African American
women at the turn of the century. Here it was, right in front of
them. I was wrong. All of the distribution companies turned it
down. . . . Again I was hearing mostly white men telling me, an
African American woman, what my people wanted to see. In
fact, they were deciding what we should be allowed to see. I
knew that was wrong. I knew they were wrong. . . . I decided to
start showing it on the festival circuit.

At the Black Light Festival in Chicago, *Daughters* sold out every showing. I went to Germany, to the Munich Film Festival and the film got a tremendous response there. Everywhere we took it, whether it was the Toronto Film Festival, the London Film Festival, or the Festival of Women in Spain, the response was the same. *Daughters of the Dust* provoked the audience. Most liked it, some did not. But it provoked them, and that made me see that I had created something important, a film that caused its audience to think and react and come to grips with their own memories.[10]

At the prestigious Sundance Festival in Utah, *Daughters* won the Best Cinematography prize for 1991. In September 1991, Kino International, a small New York City company, agreed to distribute the film. Kino hired

a new African American public relations firm, KJM3, to arrange publicity for the film. . . . Suddenly, I was appearing in national magazines and newspapers all across the country.

Daughters of the Dust opened January 15, 1992, at the Film Forum in New York. It sold out every show. The day of the opening the Coalition of One Hundred Black Women of New York gave a fashion show and reception in support of the film. I was overwhelmed. People were asking me how it felt to be the first African American woman filmmaker with a feature film in theatrical release. . . . I was moved by the emotion on the faces of the people, especially older African Americans; I was proud to be contributing to the growing power of African American filmmakers, telling the stories of our people; and I was relieved that the voices of our women were finally being heard.[11]

Daughters of the Dust was in no way a crossover film. Dash says that her intended audience for this film was "black women first, the black community second, white women third. That's who I was trying to privilege with this film. And everyone else after that."[12]

Robin Downes, formerly of Bill Cosby Productions and now an aspiring filmmaker, also creates unintimidated by Hollywood's market requirements. She says that she was a middle-class girl who felt like a foreigner when she worked on Spike Lee's *Do the Right Thing*, but the experience "opened her eyes" to the inner city.[13] Downes considers sexism more an obstacle than racism to her personal success and intends to focus her filmmaking on women's and multi-cultural issues. She is currently trying to locate financing for her screenplay, entitled *Go for It*, which tells the story of Italian, Jewish, Puerto Rican, and African American women students "coming of age" while sharing an apartment in contemporary New York City. She has already produced a twenty-minute sample of the film and takes it to various producers, distributors, and investors with the completed script.

Downes says that she is frightened that potential investors will expect only inner-city material from her simply because she is Black. Not knowing the inner city, she feels unqualified to tell its stories and resents being "typed" this way. Any "grit" found in *Go for It* is not the grit of the streets but the nitty-gritty of attaining womanhood in a sexist, racist cultural environment. Downes's focus on women's issues was in great part inspired by her work on *Do the Right Thing*, where she felt intimidated by the "masculine energy" of Lee and his crew, which she found "overpowering" and stifling. She says she knows that her work may not be commercially viable but follows the dictum "write from what you know," and the stulti-fying effects of sexism are ever present in her life.

Downes has experienced implicit sexism at the upper rung of contemporary Black film production, where bonding has proved im-portant. Like their non-Black counterparts, many Black male direc-tors and producers—among them people she has worked with, like Doug McHenry, George Jackson, Andre Harrell, and others—speak loudly and pound each other's backs as they joke and talk business. Much of the talk is of sports and women, yet when she enters the fray the conversation changes, and, Downes says, "I'm treated a 'cer-tain' way because I'm a woman." Where the conversation does not stop, Downes says, she is "left out" or "hit on" (subjected to roman-tic advances).

While she does not feel that she is consciously treated badly by Black men, the fact that they treat her with the respect men nor-mally accord women, and not "like one of the guys," is the problem. She feels she's "just not in that clique ... not less, but ... I'm a woman." Downes does not feel the same ability to connect with

Black male filmmakers that she feels with Black women, and this lack of connection with the already successful inhibits her upward climb in the film world.

In contrast to Robin Downes's approach, Monica Breckenridge, former executive director of the Black Filmmaker Foundation and former director of development for Hudlin Brothers, Inc., does not blame studios, Black men, or sexism for Black women filmmakers' lack of success. She says, rather, that Black women must wait for support from neither white-male-controlled studios nor from their already successful Black brothers. Women should not focus on exclusion but on "penetrating the system."[14] The obstacles facing Black female filmmakers are different in degree but not in kind from those faced by Black males.

> Nobody gave it to them. They weren't expecting help. They went out and said these are my terms, here's my film. I'm "in the house." And that's what Black women need to do. . . . [Financially successful Black male filmmakers] are not in a position to help women.

Breckenridge places the blame for women's limited film production success not on subject matter but on training. She says that as filmmakers she and other women "must take responsibility for [their] own career[s]." In fact, it is a "bad mentality" to ask for help. Women must develop an attitude that says, "I will not be denied." Breckenridge says that Spike Lee, for instance,

> gives himself permission. Most women don't do this. Spike takes an action and lets the chips fall where they may. [Black male producers] are on a mission which they define for themselves. . . . Women are not encouraged to take that kind of risk. . . . We need to develop the idea of being pioneers.

Leslie Harris's film *Just Another Girl on the IRT* is the second feature by an African American woman to be picked up for distribution. Harris's film, however, is attached to Miramax, a much larger, more established company than Kino International. In addition, Miramax became attached to *IRT* during postproduction and before its march on the festival circuit. This film falls very clearly into the "gritty," genre categories outlined by Grillo at New Line and seems much like a low-budget, Brooklyn-based *Girlz N the Hood*. In fact, the Miramax press write-up describes *IRT* as "the unforgettable tale of Chantel, a 'homegirl' from Brooklyn."

> Chantel's signature braids, slammin' outfits, and flip mouth scream Attitude, with a capital "A." In an environment full of perilous traps for African American teens, Chantel's attitude is a badge of survival, a method of control.[15]

The write-up goes on to say that this is the "first major commercial feature film to be released by an African American woman filmmaker." Yet the novel quality of this feature extends even to its production financing. And this might be an indication of the African American arts production future. The write-up continues:

> For Harris, it culminates a three-year saga to realistically capture the vitality of a smart, funny, sassy Black teenage girl on celluloid. The birth of the idea began when Harris created a short film sketch "Another Girl" for Planned Parenthood. "I would see teenagers on the train and would notice how other people were reacting to them," Harris recalls. "I thought it would be interesting to follow this young woman home. To have a film depict her life and what she was all about."
>
> Harris had studied film at Denison University and had produced animated shorts as a student before she moved to New York. Armed with a Bachelor of Fine Arts, she looked to sharpen her craft through a career in the advertising industry, but was not fully satisfied. Harris decided to focus all her energies on her project and began writing the script and developing the film. Between temp jobs, she flooded organizations with grant proposals. Grants trickled in from the American Film Institute, the National Endowment for the Arts, the New York State Council on the Arts, and the Jerome Foundation.

Most important for this discussion, however, is the next paragraph:

> Support also came from family and friends who believed in the project including such luminaries as Michael Moore, producer-director of *Roger and Me*, and Nelson George, an award winning author who co-wrote and produced *Strictly Business*. Another notable supporter was Terry McMillan, author of the best seller *Waiting to Exhale*, whose bold, brassy Black female characters have become her trademark. As a result, Leslie Harris has been able to make a film that Hollywood dared not do.

Leslie Harris directs Ebony Jerido in *Just Another Girl on the IRT*
(Cineaste)

Thus the entree of Leslie Harris both confirms and contradicts the Breckenridge prescription: *IRT* was made "guerrilla" style, in the Melvin Van Peebles/Spike Lee mode, but the film also received the support of other young filmmakers, both Black and white, and of a prominent new Black woman novelist. In a *New York Times* article discussing her film's presence at the 1993 Sundance Film Festival, Harris said:

> I was just tired of seeing the way black women were depicted, as wives or mothers or girlfriends or appendages. . . . All from the point of view of male directors. [Chantel's] the central character. There's no male character to validate her.[16]

It appears that African American women directors are, at last, "in the house."

Chapter 8 Unintended Collusion: The Case of Spike Lee

The latest period of Black feature film production continues the relationship between the goals of racial uplift and financial success attempted in the Du Bois/Washington feature, *The Birth of a Race*, through the many films of Oscar Micheaux and Melvin Van Peebles's *Sweetback*. These filmmakers considered the political at least as important as, if not more important than, the aesthetic purpose of their work. In fact, the word *artist*, as usually applied to filmmakers such as David Lean or Francis Ford Coppola, seems inappropriate for most African American filmmakers. Whether they like it or not, the fact that most of their films comment on racism, sexism, poverty, oppression, and other social ills has caused critics and everyday viewers to respond more to the implicit social commentary than to the artistry of their films.

These new Black filmmakers see themselves as warriors putting forth a particularly Black point of view. Trey Ellis, for example, praises *She's Gotta Have It* "because it was so true to the black"; on the other hand, he says, singers Whitney Houston and Lionel Ritchie have "transformed themselves into cultural-mulattos, assimilationist nightmares; neutered mutations instead of thriving hybrids." Ellis throws down the political gauntlet: "Nationalist pride continues to be one of the strongest forces in the black community . . . It is not an apolitical, art-for-art's-sake fantasy. We realize that despite this current buppie artist boom, most black Americans have seldom had it worse."[1]

The tradition of the African American film artist as responsive to the needs of African Americans who have it worse continues. Generally, the new Black filmmakers see their struggle for success as

(*Left to right*) Author Jesse Rhines; attorney Stephen Barnes;
writer Trey Ellis and his wife, Erika; Susan Land; director
Reginald Hudlin; Michele Clayborne *(Jesse Rhines)*

a part of the struggle waged by the rest of African America from the
time of slavery to the present. Warrington Hudlin has said that "historically, the Black Filmmaker Foundation is a product of the political and artistic consciousness that developed in the late 60's and
early 70's. Many of its affiliated filmmakers received their film
education and training through university admissions policies and
government programs that targeted Blacks and other so-called minorities."[2] Many of the young Black filmmakers who are "making it"
today are products of affirmative action and other programs designed specifically to aid development of Americans of color. In fact,
it was the inability to gain entree into the feature film industry that
led to the creation of BFF.

> When I came out of film school my goal was to become a cre-
> ative artist and almost by default did I become an organizer. I
> realized that my creative aspirations could not be successfully
> pursued in the face of the institution of racism that has disen-
> franchised Black people as filmmakers. So in order to have the
> opportunity, and for all of us to have the opportunity, someone
> had to do the work of organizing in our collective interest to fill
> the gaps that hinder our being successful filmmakers. Gaps like
> distribution, exhibitions, and access to our work and each
> other.[3]

Warrington Hudlin and Reginald Hudlin (*on left*) confer with
a cinematographer and actress Tracy Johns during the shooting
of a 1987 music video *(Jesse Rhines)*

Yet, as a mere handful of new Black filmmakers have found financial success, they have done so within a context of decreased opportunity for poor Blacks who live within America's central cities.
What is the value of that success for the more than one-third of the
African American community that has not been so lucky?

Spike Lee remains the best-known African American filmmaker.
He is conscious that he has become something of an intellectual
conduit between that 30 percent deemed the Black urban underclass
and those Americans whose social and economic status is at least
middle class. Beyond the aesthetic value of Spike Lee's films, how
important is the information Lee conveys to and about Blacks stuck
in the inner city? Response to this question is presented not in the
theater but in television news programs, newspapers, news magazines, and business and scholarly journals. Unlike most filmmakers,
Spike Lee can be found on many media channels normally concerned with dissemination of more mundane information of a political, sociological, or economic nature than with film or art. Why do
these channels invite Lee, a filmmaker, to speak about the Black

urban underclass and not about film? What is the nature of the information Spike Lee provides, and how does it function in the American political and economic contexts?

Spike Lee as Information Conduit

In the African filmmaking diaspora, there is no better-known film practitioner, or cineaste, than Spike Lee.[4] Yet artistry is not the foundation of this renown. Spike Lee is most honored for his courage and audacity in presenting "a" view of "a" segment of the Black world that is largely held in common by "a" segment of the Black world. Additionally, this renown stems from Lee's presentation of this singular view to two, nearly mutually exclusive audiences. One is the various Black, globally dispersed communities, where this singular view serves a function akin to an essential "main dish" at a family reunion: it is something around which the various communities may focus and investigate the concept of unity among the communities (despite the fact that all present may dislike the main dish). The other is these communities' perceived common enemy(ies), who are, primarily, people of the European diaspora who have, in the past or currently, collectively and/or singly, conquered, dominated, dispersed, and/or influenced those of the African diaspora.

This concept of unity that Lee enunciates is a kind of nationalist cultural weltanschauung, porous and open to argument and debate by everyone and anyone. Even his first feature film, *She's Gotta Have It*, while not ostensibly a political work, was conceived and received by Black people the world over as a heretofore rare presentation of Black cultural norms, traditions, customs, or practices.[5] In general, Black reaction was that this film presented a valid representation of a segment of Black cultural life. Generally held opinions such as this demonstrate an element of a Black national cultural character distinguishable from that of persons who do not share Black national culture. While national culture or national character is difficult to define, it is often easy to recognize. Despite the fact, for example, that members of both the French and American nations eat chicken, the cuisines of these two nations are distinct. Both

Anglo and African American men court women. Yet the styles and particulars of these two nations' courtship rituals are distinguishable, though not mutually exclusive. For reasons of his narrative focus on such distinctions, Spike Lee might be called a purveyor of a Black, perhaps even Afrocentric, national cultural identity.[6]

Although Spike Lee is broadly admired among African Americans, it is white America—and the media that serves it—that has given him "real" stardom. Chris Wallace of ABC News called Lee in 1990 "a multimedia conglomerate these days: promoting his fourth movie, already producing his fifth while, in his spare time, cutting his latest TV commercials. At age thirty-three, he is the most powerful black filmmaker ever. But he's certain the white power structure in Hollywood is just waiting for him to fail."[7]

His detractors are forced to acknowledge his stature even as they use it against him. In a 1991 *Critical Inquiry* article, Jerome Christensen accused Lee of using the "Wall of Fame" in Sal's pizza parlor to elevate himself to the level of Malcolm X, Nelson Mandela, and Michael Jordan. Christensen claimed that "the final cause of *Do the Right Thing* is the manifestation of Spike Lee's celebrity [which] is the capital that sustains Forty Acres and a Mule Productions."[8] *Esquire*'s Pete Hamill has said that "part of the Spike Lee miracle is that he has managed to attract white audiences to movies about black people without sentimentalizing the agonizing American problems with race."[9] *Business Week* magazine commented, "Spike Lee does a lot of things right," and it has labeled him "a multimedia star and marketing phenomenon."[10] Obviously, such praise is the result of Lee's marketability not to the Black community but to a mass audience mostly made up of whites. The question arises, then, what makes Spike Lee such a media star?

Although he is broadly accepted as being a tremendous and charismatic talent (as is, for instance, Eddie Murphy), Lee's mass appeal and newsworthiness are derived primarily from his position as champion and expositor of the Black underclass. It is white people's association of his media persona with the popularized public policy and academic debate on African America's lopsided post–civil rights development that attracts the mass audience.

Even before *She's Gotta Have It* was made, Spike Lee was an acknowledged talent in the art of filmmaking. He had won a Student Academy Award presented by the Academy of Motion Picture Arts and Sciences for his NYU thesis film, *Joe's Bed-Stuy Barber Shop: We Cut Heads*. After *She's Gotta Have It* won big at the San Francisco Film Festival, Island Pictures acquired the right to distribute the film. *She's Gotta Have It* subsequently won the Prix de la Jeunesse at the Cannes Film Festival, and both the box office and American film critics piled on the praise. Pauline Kael of *The New Yorker* observed:

> And Lee himself is endowed with something more than training and imagination: he has what for want of a better term is called "a film sense." It's an instinct for how to make a movie move—for how much motion there should be in a shot, for how fast to cut the shots, for how to make them flow into each other rhythmically. . . . (John Sayles has many gifts but not a film sense—he doesn't gain anything as an artist by using film—and this probably explains why Ernest Dickerson's work for him on "The Brother from Another Planet" looks stiff and pedestrian).[11]

This is high praise, especially considering Lee is being measured against John Sayles, who opted out of the Hollywood establishment to make a number of well-received independent productions. Later Spike Lee productions, such as *Do the Right Thing*, have received similar artistic acclaim.

Charm is also an acknowledged factor in Spike Lee's popularity. However, early mention of this quality was tied to Mars Blackmon, the character Lee played in *She's Gotta Have It*. In critics' comments on this character, we see the emergence of Lee's association with the Black underclass. The film itself seems to have originally disappointed *New Republic* critic Stanley Kauffman, for he commented: "The film makes some promises that it doesn't keep. We first see some still shots of Bedford-Stuyvesant, but they are misleading: the story is about middle-class blacks."[12] Yet Lee's character was not received as middle class. David Denby of *New York* magazine labeled Mars "a scrawny little pest on a ten-speed bike . . . an unemployed loser [yet] when he's onscreen, he brings a charge of comic energy to what he's doing that dazzles the audience."[13] In the *New York Times Magazine*, Stuart Mieher called Mars "a rapping street kid

John Turturro, Danny Aiello, and Richard Edson as a pizzeria owner and
his sons in *Do the Right Thing* (Cineaste/David Lee)

who joked his way into [Nola Darling's] bed and stole scene after
scene."[14] Through this affable character, white audiences were introduced to both Spike Lee and, by inference, to similar rapping, poor,
Black street kids. Mars made them seem approachable and, perhaps,
potentially worthy of respect. Jack Barth said, "It takes some self-
assurance for a director to prance around on-screen with a pair of
panties on his head. Without Spike's formidable charm, how could
he get away with putting a line in his movie that describes his
slightly elephant-headed lead actor as a '16-piece Chicken McNug-
get-head'?"[15]

Thus at the beginning, Spike Lee's charm was delivered by Mars
Blackmon, Lee's funny, approachable, likable creation. Since Mars
was perceived as a member of the Black urban underclass, Spike
Lee's popular persona was so linked as well. Rather than attempt to
change this perception, Lee purposely enhanced and built upon his
identification with the Black urban poor. While this can be seen as
a niche-marketing strategy, Lee grounds such identification in the
ideology of racial uplift and personal experience vicariously gained
in childhood.

By the mid-1980s, white America had heard about and wanted to know more about the Black urban underclass. Though frequently featured in news stories on crime, teen parenthood, welfare, and so on, this group was still enigmatic for the mass audience. As a result of the success of the civil rights movement itself, whites had seen more Blacks than ever move into the public eye. Some had even acquired positions of seeming power and influence. Yet there persisted a cry that opportunities for general Black advancement were foreclosed. Crime statistics, poverty statistics, employment statistics—and those dangerous-looking Black boys and men whom desegregation now allowed to roam downtown—provided clear evidence that large numbers of Blacks were not advancing as expected.

Scholarly realization that the "Black community" was bifurcating socially and economically was crystallized in the late 1970s. William Julius Wilson's *The Declining Significance of Race* (1978) catalyzed intense debate on the continued efficacy of civil rights–inspired approaches to increasing urban deprivation.[16] He defined as Black underclass those regions

> populated almost exclusively by the most disadvantaged segments of the black urban community, that heterogeneous grouping of families and individuals who are outside the mainstream of the American occupational system. Included in this group are individuals who lack training and skills and either experience long-term unemployment or are not members of the labor force, individuals who are engaged in street crime and other forms of aberrant behavior, and families that experience long-term spells of poverty and/or welfare dependency.[17]

In *The Declining Significance of Race*, Wilson calculated their numbers at about 31 percent (7.5 million people) of America's Black population.[18] In 1986, when *She's Gotta Have It* was released, popular interest in the Black underclass was increasing. In 1989, Spike Lee addressed the underclass directly in the film *Do the Right Thing*. On July 6, 1989, the entire ABC News program *Nightline* was devoted to this film, and Lee was one of the program's guests. In the program's introduction, ABC News anchor Forrest Sawyer posed the question:

> Who would have guessed a modestly budgeted film about rac-

ism, set in a black neighborhood of Brooklyn, would be a national hit. . . . This film is making Americans listen and talk, even argue, about one of the most painful problems in our society.[19]

Later in the program, ABC's Jeff Greenfield said America was more impressed by Lee's ideological and political view than by his artistry:

> By almost unanimous consent *Do the Right Thing* is a terrific movie, humorous, moving, compelling. But that's not why it's drawn more attention than any film in recent memory. It's because of what Spike Lee is saying, about the explosive question of racism.[20]

Next day, Spike Lee was praised as the most newsworthy "Person of the Week" on ABC's *World News Tonight.*

Although his first and second feature releases, *She's Gotta Have It* and *School Daze,* targeted the middle-class Black rather than the Black urban underclass, and despite the fact that he admits of no professional experience in the social science arena, Spike Lee's media persona has been steeped in underclass social and political issues from the beginning. The name of his production company, Forty Acres and a Mule, is an indication of his identification with Black disenfranchisement. In 1987, he commented that one message he wanted to deliver was that "we're not all hanging around in the ghetto, shooting up, selling crack."[21] Lee simultaneously charms while challenging white America to confront its continuing racism when he says things like this:

> To end [*Do the Right Thing*] with Sal and Mookie kissing each other, holding hands, singing "We are the World," "Don't Worry, Be Happy," "We're all God's children," " It doesn't matter if we're Black, white, purple or green, we're all the same inside." That's bullshit. It's complete bullshit and that's what gets me mad about this whole American myth, that it doesn't matter what color you are, creed or nationality, and as long as you're American, you'll be treated the same and viewed the same. That's a lie. It's the biggest lie ever perpetrated on the people in the history of mankind. None of my work is going to reflect that.[22]

And in response to criticism that *Do the Right Thing* made whites uncomfortable, despite their desire to learn from it, he responded:

> How do you think Black people have felt for 80 years watching stuff like *Birth of a Nation* . . . and we go on and on. Black people have had to live under this thing for 400 years. If white people have to squirm for two hours watching this film, that's great. I think it's a good kind of squirming, because for the most part the movies today are just mindless entertainment; they don't make you think. We made this film so we could put the spotlight on racism and say that everything is NOT okay, that this is not the land of milk and honey and truth and justice. We should stop hiding from the issue of racism.[23]

Spike Lee has taken a public position on the side of the Black disadvantaged despite the fact that he has never been one of them. "Just because I was brought up in a middle-class background," he says, "does not mean I should dissociate myself from the black underclass. . . . I think that's one of the problems we have as a people . . . that the Black middle-class has abandoned the lower class."[24] In an August 29, 1989, *Nightline* discussion entitled "Black in White America," Lee demonstrated that he knew and identified with less fortunate neighbors from early childhood:

> Both my parents were home, and my friends would come over. They were amazed that both of my parents lived with us. We were thought of as Martians, it was something so foreign to them. And I think that the reason why I'm able to do what I'm doing today is because I had both my parents there to raise me, and that makes a difference, a lot of difference.[25]

Amazingly, despite frequent allusion to heroic African American scholars of years gone by, such as sociologist W.E.B. Du Bois and Booker T. Washington, Lee admits never having heard of Wilson, the contemporary African American sociologist policymakers most associate with the characters portrayed in Lee's own films. Asked if he had read any of William Julius Wilson, Lee replied, "Who? No." Lee says that he never studied social sciences in college, "just literature."[26] Lee's approach to the underclass is that of the artist intent on expressing his feelings rather than the scholar intending to explicate a social phenomenon.

In response to editor-publisher Bob Guccione Jr.'s offer to edit an entire issue of *Spin* magazine, Lee declared, "It would be the Black-est issue they've ever had."[27] Lee accepted, and it was. The issue contained interviews conducted by Lee with Eddie Murphy and the Reverend Al Sharpton—a person heretofore vilified by the white media for his activities on the part of Tawana Brawley, Yusef Hawk-ins, and others whom Blacks viewed as directly oppressed by the American police and justice systems.

These interviews are insightful and conducted with tremendous compassion. The reader learns a great deal about both interviewees and about Lee's own feelings about the point of view each repre-sents. For example, Eddie Murphy is not seen, and does not claim, to speak on behalf of any Black people other than himself. Yet we find that he admires Lee for speaking out:

> The scariest thing about you to me—and the scariest thing is the thing I admire most about you—is that every black person who really stood up and said, "Fuck it, I'm about this," got dissed, killed, fucked over—everybody, from Dr. King to Ali, you know? It's like, they fuck you over and shit, so my thing is, I commend you on that—that you say, "This is what my shit is about, you know?" My politics are much more covert. I am very black and I have a very strong black consciousness but I am about gradual change and dialogue that is much more civil.[28]

Readers learned from the Al Sharpton interview that, contrary to popular opinion, both Lee and Sharpton share more than a simplis-tic understanding of the plight of Blacks in America. Sharpton is re-vealed as more like a child prodigy than a flash-in-the-pan. Unlike most activists he has been associated with the movement to improve living conditions for Blacks since he was ten years old and has been close to Adam Clayton Powell and Jesse Jackson since his teens. For his part, Lee reveals a sophisticated understanding of a most nega-tive impact of integration: the destruction of Black businesses that had thrived during segregation. We also learn that Lee believes Blacks should demand more of Black entertainers by refusing to buy records by artists who "make videos with white women in every single video, no sisters."[29] Such statements indicate clearly that Spike Lee sees some reciprocal social responsibility between entertainment artists and audiences.

Spike Lee has articulated and exposed the view from the Black urban underclass at a time when whites are thirsty for information about this group. The device of the affable, approachable, comic Mars Blackmon may have provided entree to white living rooms, but since he's been there, Spike has forthrightly laid the least privileged Blacks' cards on the table.

The Nature of Lee's Information

What is meant by the American "political and economic contexts"? In essence, what is meant here is two aspects of the ability to accomplish goals defined in terms of (1) getting large numbers of people to do a particular thing as opposed to some other thing and (2) having the ability to access, distribute, and generally manipulate resources in the perennial environment of resource scarcity. The ultimate ability to function in either of these environments is described as the ability to wage war and, in a global context, is held by the State, broadly defined. However, within each State, contestation over these issues is ultimately political and is defined by statutes supported and enforced by those having the ability to make their choices and preferences binding on the rest of society. It is this "binding" function that undergirds the media's importance and significance in society. The media defines what things bind members of society together and relates seemingly disparate elements one to the other. In particular, the media relates potentially adversarial interests and locates common ground between them. It defines mutually beneficial links between upper and lower classes as well as between master and slave races. Without the intervention of the media, white rule of African-born slaves would have been an even more bloody situation than it was. Because whites were able to appeal to slaves' reason, on occasion, and persuade them through scripture, punishment demonstrations, and other means that Africans were inherently inferior to Europeans, not only was the potential for slave revolts reduced but, in many cases, slaves actually betrayed their revolutionary brothers to their masters.

In the case of economic and social classes, the media also plays an amelioratory role in purveying the message that the upper classes are accessible to anyone. Examples are provided of recent immigrants and formerly poverty-stricken workers who have risen to become wealthy and influential people. The media ties the classes together by demonstrating that the upper and lower classes are the same in terms of the individuals who make them up. At this level, in fact, they are not classes at all but people each seeking the same goals and with their own individual assets and obstacles to face. The media does not emphasize either race-to-race or class-to-class relations but individual-to-individual relations and, in this way, performs its binding function as it demonstrates an inherent equality between all persons in society.

How do we assess Spike Lee's function as a binding agent of the media? After all, there are two ways the binding function can be performed: as a partner who is embraced, honored, and rewarded by society or as an enemy against whom society unites and whom it seeks to punish.

A significant function Spike Lee performs is to define the Black urban underclass and make it both more familiar and less threatening to white Americans. Does the definition and threat diminishment he provides, however, augur well for poor Blacks, for whites, or for both? Much of what Lee says in the media has to do with historical sociological commentary from persons such as Booker T. Washington, Malcolm X, and Jesse Jackson, among others. Their positions on the right to jobs, antipoverty solutions, and the liberation of African Americans are well known. How does what Lee says, both verbally and on film, compare with their statements as useful information?

JOBS VERSUS DISCIPLINE

The works of French scholar Michel Foucault are used to explain how highly developed countries handled the post–World War II transition from modern, industrial societies to postmodern, postindustrial societies. Industrial nations depend on factories employing thousands of low-skilled workers to produce manufactured goods. Postindustrial societies, such as the United States, began getting rid of these factories (deindustrializing) in the 1950s and prefer to import goods manufactured by lower-paid workers in other countries.

Most scholars and policy analysts agree that local deindustrial-ization causes workers to lose current jobs. There is, however, much debate about the impact of such job loss on the local social environment. Wilson and conservative social critic Charles Murray, for example, take opposing positions as to whether a lack of individual discipline or lack of jobs is the primary plague afflicting the Black urban poor. Murray sees crime, youthful, out-of-wedlock pregnancy, and increasing welfare statistics as indicating a deficit in individual self-discipline, while Wilson sees them as indicating a lack of available good jobs.

In contrast to both these scholars, however, Michel Foucault sees the problem as historic and integral to the development of European political and economic systems. For Foucault, the problem originated hundreds of years ago, in attempts by an emerging capitalist class to get ordinary people to leave other pursuits and work in the capitalists' factories. Because this nascent working class tended to avoid work and not to care about the quality of its work, capitalists instituted continuous laborer observation and disciplinary methods already successful in prisons to keep workers on their toes. As factories proved more and more profitable, they, and constantly improving methods to observe and improve discipline, spread so thoroughly through Western society that workers were expected to arrive at factories with certain disciplinary habits already ingrained. In fact, "appropriate," disciplined behavior became a hallmark of Western society as each individual was now expected to apply self-control at every waking moment. It is this discipline, Foucault says, that "makes" individuals.

> It is the specific technique of a power that regards individuals both as objects and as instruments of its exercise. It is not a triumphant power [like a king or a policeman imposing his will], which because of its own excess can pride itself on its omnipotence; it is a modest, suspicious power, which functions as a calculated, but permanent economy. . . . The exercise of discipline presupposes a mechanism that coerces by means of observation; an apparatus in which the techniques that make it possible to see induce effects of power, and in which, conversely, the means of coercion make those on whom they are applied clearly visible.[30]

Self-discipline is applied according to the dictates of a norm each individual learns from parents, school, church, and other civil institutions. Why is this norm established and applied? There are two reasons. First, following the norm keeps one "out of trouble." Second, those who best follow the norm, or improve on it, are "rewarded" with either jobs or some other form of security. "Staying out of trouble" and "accepting a job," however, are encouraged by civil institutions at the behest of average, middle-class, and other American taxpayers who, through the State apparatus, must punish those who do not stay out of trouble and supply a reasonable level of security for those who do not accept jobs or otherwise provide for their own security. The current outcry against the American "homeless"—undisciplined individuals who defy the norm by not providing for their own security—illustrates this latter requirement.

Average taxpayers, however, are not the only ones who appeal for the State to encourage self-discipline. The capitalist class, which manufactures and distributes the nation's goods and services, requires self-disciplined workers in its employ. In fact, when taxpayers refuse to fund effective schools, the capitalists will create schools in-house and train their own workers. Self-discipline is a major part of the ideology of all developed countries, including the United States. It is also a major part of the ideology of the dominant, Anglo-Saxon, American culture under which African Americans of all classes live and with which they are expected and encouraged to comply.

In present-day America, however, this approach does not work for the underclass. School, church, and family fail to inculcate the values of self-discipline among inner-city nonwhite populations. The main indicator of this failure is delinquency, which, those in government and social work organizations contend, results in crime. In centuries past, punishment by torture and cruel death were the State's reaction to large- and small-scale undisciplined behavior. However, public morality—as codified in the U.S. Constitution—forbids such actions now, so other methods are used.

During slavery undisciplined African Americans were whipped, maimed, or summarily killed by whites. During Jim Crow, undisciplined Blacks were lynched or tarred and feathered. Today, the undisciplined among the underclass must be made visible and manageable by government. This is accomplished by putting so many underclass Blacks behind bars that a decidedly disproportionate share of the African American male population is in jail at any one time. In their study and statistical compilation on African America, Yale University economist Gerald Jaynes and Cornell University sociologist Robin Williams Jr. note that "blacks are arrested, convicted, and imprisoned for criminal offenses at rates much higher than are whites. Currently, blacks account for nearly one-half of all prison inmates in the United States; thus, blacks' representation in prisons is about 4 times their representation in the general population."[31] This is a consistent application of the new Euro-American morality, which supports imprisonment of lawbreakers over torture and corporal punishment. Murray argues that welfare and other social services actually encourage continued undisciplined behavior rather than discourage it.

William Julius Wilson takes quite a different view of the problem. According to him, members of the underclass do not become self-disciplined because there is no incentive: there are no jobs in the inner city that either provide a living wage or significantly reward discipline for those with exceptional capabilities. To take advantage of the financial benefits and incentives of a global economy, capitalists have moved manufacturing and production abroad or to suburban areas difficult for the inner-city poor to reach. Takaki, who shares Wilson's viewpoint, says:

> The last three decades have witnessed radical economic transformations and the growth of a Black underclass . . . families in desperate need because of economic changes. . . . The movement of plants and offices to the suburbs has isolated inner city Blacks in terms of employment.
>
> Meanwhile, Blacks also suffered from the devastating effects of the "deindustrialization of America." . . . Tens of millions of American workers have lost their jobs due to the relocation of production in low-wage countries like South Korea and Mexico. [In this] army of displaced workers has been a disproportionately large number of Blacks.[32]

The removal of jobs from inner cities has been exacerbated by continued in-migration of poorly educated Blacks. Wilson says, "Blacks constituted approximately 23 percent of the population of central cities in 1983, but they were 43 percent of the poor in these cities."[33] Changes in immigration laws halted continued concentrations of Asians and other nonwhites in central cities. This

> enabled those already here to solidify networks of ethnic contacts and occupy particular occupational niches in small, relatively stable communities. . . . However, black migration to the urban North continued in substantial numbers for several decades. . . . Only a small part of a group's total work force can be absorbed in [occupational niches] when the group's population increases rapidly or is a sizable proportion of the total population.[34]

In addition, during the Cold War, industries remaining in the United States increasingly became military and information oriented. Such high-tech enterprises require very few workers compared with traditional manufacturing, and these must have skill complements too high-tech for underclass members' level of education. As manufacturers have run away from increasingly nonwhite inner cities, low-paying service sector jobs—for example, in fast food outlets—are the only ones generally available to inner-city workers.

Why is nothing done about the lack of jobs in these areas? The reasons for this are twofold: (1) there are few financial incentives to provide jobs in these inner cities, and (2) few people know or believe that lack of jobs is the reason for the undisciplined behavior. As to the first reason, the very definition of an underclass requires that the capitalist class has no way of making money from its labor. Even though the only culturally valued means to rise above poverty legitimately in the American system is individual achievement through labor, if no one is willing to buy your labor, no one is there to pay you to labor. This situation is complicated by the "success" of the civil rights movement's integrationist approach, which still encourages entrepreneurial and middle-class Blacks to leave traditionally Black areas. The flight of this group has left inner cities unattractive environments for capitalistic investment.

As to the second reason for a continued lack of jobs in inner cities, a debate rages in academic, governmental, and popular arenas as to whether this or something else is the underlying rationale for the lack of self-discipline among the underclass. While policymakers generally rely on scholarly journals, newspapers, and offices of state to carry on their debate, the average American taxpayer considers this issue through programs such as *Donahue* and *Nightline*, popular magazines like *Premiere*, and even the movie theater. It is the popular media, such as television and movies, that takes on the task of explaining phenomena such as "the underclass" to the average American taxpayer. This is an important role for the media because the cost of eliminating an underclass—which produces no wealth with which to improve its own condition—would have to be borne by the capitalist class and/or middle-class American taxpayers. What the average American understands of the underclass will affect his or her willingness to either allow the underclass to continue or intervene in the interest of its members.

This is where the efforts and works of Spike Lee enter the debate. On the issue of the impact manufacturing's relocation to suburbs and developing countries has on inner-city jobs, Lee said, "That affects white workers too. If your job flies out the country . . . [you're in bad shape]." When asked specifically about closed factories in Brooklyn where parents of people now on the street used to work, Lee said:

> Yeah, I can't imagine Brooklyn being any different from the rest of the United States. The economy is down, businesses are moving. In New York City a lot of businesses are moving to New Jersey and Connecticut and leaving. Wonder Bread just closed recently. . . . Those people had jobs. They were lower middle class at least. They were working people. But the underclass, they work too. Work two, three jobs. I think it's a myth to say everybody in the lower class is on welfare. That's not true.[35]

In fact, here Lee has recognized a major problem: people of the underclass must "work two, three jobs"—similar to the one worked by Mookie in *Do the Right Thing*—in the low-paid service industry to earn a living wage. Although his job at Sal's seems steady, Mookie is underemployed and unable to care for his family. Lee sees and understands the problem but generalizes it to the whole society. He does not recognize that while anyone, regardless of race, can be put

Mookie (Spike Lee) shares a tender moment with Tina (Rosie Perez)
in *Do the Right Thing* *(Cineaste/David Lee)*

out of work by runaway shops, the Black urban underclass is con-
fined to communities in a way that focuses and concentrates disad-
vantages more than in other communities. Housing segregation and
lack of standard education, combined with the removal of develop-
mental resources, such as bank loans, from their communities leaves
underemployed urban Blacks stuck in increasingly degraded, geopo-
litically separated communities. The resultant financial and social
degradation allows Black and non-Black auto insurance and other
service providers headquartered elsewhere to then redline underclass areas.

This is the real-life context for the young Blacks depicted in
Lee's films. Jaynes and Williams presented findings in *A Common
Destiny* (which President George Bush called a "monumental study"
and the *New York Times* deemed "the most substantial compilation
and analysis of black social, political, and economic trends since
World War II") that indicate that Black youths aged sixteen to
twenty-four and living in the poorest areas of central cities are
"much more likely to be unemployed and less likely to be employed
than white youths or all black youths. They tend to have slightly

lower wages than other youths and they work fewer weeks per year. In addition, those youths have far worse family backgrounds than others. One-third of them live in public housing; almost one-half of them have a family member on welfare. Only 28 percent of them have an adult man in their household."[36]

What was Mookie's salary? Why wasn't Mars employed? Again in 1980, 71 percent of African Americans lived in the inner city while 66 percent of whites lived in the suburbs.[37] Simply by residential patterns, whites and Blacks, in general, have different employment experiences. In addition, many of the factories that left Blacks jobless in central cities moved to the suburbs, where they employed the white workers living there. Wonder Bread, for example, closed its Brooklyn bakery and consolidated operations in Queens, New York.

Black Americans are not only unemployed in increasing numbers, but more and more are unemployable, superfluous to the labor market. This condition is the essence of the underclass and leads to the conclusion that the underclass will be permanent until its members die off. What are the employment expectations for Mookie's son, Hector? Mookie's salary will never send him to college even if the education he gets in local schools prepares him.

What does Lee tell American taxpayers about the origin of the underclass? Lee sees the underclass as having arisen from "federal cutbacks: Eight years of Reaganomics. Four years of Bush. Poverty programs being cut and slashed or eliminated altogether. It's a vicious cycle. People are losing hope. That might be the biggest thing: hopelessness."[38] This allusion to "hopelessness" born of Reaganomics does indicate that Lee does not place the entire blame for the underclass condition on individual African Americans or on Blacks as a group. In *She's Gotta Have It*, the film that introduced Americans to the Black urban underclass and to Spike Lee in the character of Mars Blackmon, Nola Darling has invited her three lovers to Thanksgiving dinner.

NOLA
I invited all of you fools. Shut up and eat.

GREER
She's right. Let's enjoy this day. We have a lot to be thankful for.

MARS
Like what?

GREER
Our health. Our careers.

MARS
I've been unemployed for two years. (*rapping*) Fifty-dollar sneakers and I got no job. Tell me how to do it when times is hard.[39]

Clearly, Lee wants the audience to view Greer and Mars as identifying with different class backgrounds. It is also clear that the audience is expected to laugh at, not with, Mars's undisciplined behavior exemplified in buying fifty-dollar sneakers when he does not have a job. The audience is led to ask such questions as: Where did he get the fifty dollars? How does he eat? Did he steal the bicycle he rides? How could a nonworking person buy a necklace, which he claims is real gold, with his name in huge, ostentatious lettering? Criminality is implied, and the audience is led to question Mars's earlier claim of "I pay my own way," made when he suggested he would like to move into Nola's apartment.

Lee does not answer any of these questions. We also never learn why Mars has been out of a job for two years or whether or not he has been looking for a job. Mars Blackmon's character symbolizes the Black urban underclass, but Lee never explains where that underclass came from or how the conditions of poverty under which the underclass lives might be alleviated. The impression left on the viewing audience, however, is consistent with Charles Murray's contention that lack of self-discipline is the cause of underclass poverty. The audience saw no one force Mars to pay an exorbitant amount for his sneakers or gold chain. The disciplined person would have saved that money for future investment in a business venture or continued education. Lee's depiction of the underclass does not encourage American taxpayers to support improvement among members of the underclass but rather to punish them even more.

Yet, while *Do the Right Thing* received tremendous media and critical attention, few critics more than hinted at Lee's silence as to the origin of and solutions to the Black underclass dilemma. In the journal *Black Scholar*, Robert Chrisman went furthest in addressing this omission. Chrisman said that *"Do the Right Thing* leaves one with a melange of contradictory and, at times, confused messages that suggest that the film has no clear vision of racial relation in a metropole, even as a problematic. . . . And it does not pose the question, '*Why* are these blacks unemployed?'"[40] Chrisman allowed his question to be taken rhetorically by neglecting to provide possible answers in this essay, but at least he is not far from the mark.

By contrast, J. Hoberman, in the *Village Voice*, merely stated that "you can't avoid having a point of view" about this film. "But the real issue," he said, "is not the absence of drugs or street crime; the real issue is racial solidarity. . . . *Do the Right Thing* presents no essential divisions within the black community."[41] Is this a criticism or a pat on the back? Division within the Black community is something the white community has encouraged and even forced on Blacks since slavery. Do Hoberman's comments continue this tradition by encouraging African America's media makers to make intraracial division a part of their message as well?

In the *Los Angeles Times*, Sheila Benson said that

> Lee's intent is no less than a behind-the-scenes guide to a racial conflagration. . . . What Lee is showing is a series of abrasive incidents, trivial by themselves that, combined with soaring heat and in a climate of oppressiveness, finally ignite. In fact, Lee suggests that the actual point from which the fury builds is petty, if not ridiculous: Buggin' Out's demands that Sal put a few black faces up there with Sinatra, Pacino, DeNiro and DiMaggio in the pizzeria's fly-specked, Italian-American wall of fame. . . . Lee's point is that, like the Howard Beach tragedy in New York or the case of Vincent Chin in Detroit, what follows comes from a mixture of fear, sociology, economics and feeling buried so deep that those who carry them would deny they exist.[42]

While Benson did mention sociology and economics, she left it up to readers to figure out where in these two huge fields of intellectual endeavor the problem *actually* exists. Chrisman at least pinpointed unemployment for his readers.

Vincent Canby of the *New York Times*, probably the most-read critic of *Do the Right Thing*, did to his reader precisely what he accused Lee of doing to his viewers. He said the film "is the chronicle of a bitter racial confrontation that leaves one man dead and a neighborhood destroyed. The ending is shattering and maybe too ambiguous for its own good."[43] Canby's critique is too incomplete for the good of American audiences. Since he and Benson both acknowledge Lee's focus on racism as the film's leitmotif, the question should be, does the film locate racism's origin, and how is racism manifest? Lee has an advanced education and has lived more than three decades under a racist regime. His insights on such questions may hint at how racism can be attacked in a nonambiguous manner. Unfortunately, however, the impression left by these critics is the same as that left by Spike Lee: racism is an irrational, individual pathology. The racism that stifles and oppresses nonwhites, however, is actually the product of a system of economic relations that pits one group against another in the interest of singular economic gain. Most individual racists, like Sal's son Vito, are only small fry, the relief of whose personal racism will have little appreciable impact on the life chances of the underclass members featured in *Do the Right Thing*.

SOLUTIONS: DEATH VERSUS PROGRAMS

The solution to the underclass problem from Murray's point of view is "white popular wisdom," that is, to be harsher on the individual: eliminate welfare, unemployment insurance, Medicaid, and food stamps. Stronger focus on "law and order," which translates into stiffer jail sentences (at minimum) for offenders, is encouraged. These policies would force the underclass to have fewer children and take advantage of opportunities available within the general system of American capitalism. Such a solution profile is also consistent with the view of Shelby Steele, who locates the origin of the underclass in the absence of "middle-class values . . . the work ethic, the importance of education, the value of property ownership, of respectability, of 'getting ahead,' of stable family life, of initiative, of self-reliance, et cetera," which, he says, are "raceless and even assimilationist. They urge us toward participation in the American mainstream, toward integration, toward a strong identification with the society, and toward the entire constellation of qualities that are implied in the word individualism. These values are almost rules for how to prosper in a democratic, free enterprise society that admires and rewards individual effort."[44]

Takaki challenges this position, saying that Murray has missed the forest by focusing too narrowly on the trees. According to Murray's parable of the imaginary unmarried couple, Phyllis and Harold, by 1970 AFDC standards, a Phyllis with a child receives more income from welfare plus food stamps if she remains unmarried than she will receive either married with Harold's minimum wage income or married and living on welfare. The decision not to marry and to accept welfare is a rational one for Phyllis. Takaki says, however, that the problem is not the availability of welfare but the low wages Harold is forced to accept.[45] Murray's proposition assumes minimum wages for African American men and financial dependence on men by African American women. The real problem pointed to is that large numbers of African Americans cannot find decent-paying employment. If welfare were not available, these people still would not have high-paying jobs and, given the dearth of investment monies available to low-income people generally, would not be able to borrow money for business or education investment. Thus the Takaki-Wilson solution to the problem of the underclass is to provide more jobs in inner-city communities even at taxpayer expense.

Spike Lee does not believe that direct contributions from all African Americans will be successful in eliminating the problem of the Black urban underclass. "You have to get people who have money, [accountability,] and time and work on it from there. Anytime you try to get everybody, it's not gonna work." When asked about the feasibility of separatism for African Americans or a subnational, semigovernmental body to minister to the needs of Blacks in the communities where they currently live, Lee said to both, "That's never gonna happen." He agreed with the suggestion that African Americans must contend with whites living proximate to and among them for the long term. "Let's be honest," Lee said, "nobody's getting on the North Star line going back to Africa. Look at the boat they sold Marcus [Garvey]. I'm not knocking him. I'm just talking about reality."[46]

Lee's films present a solution to the underclass problem more worthy of the artist than the scholar, and this one is being practiced in the underclass community itself. *Jungle Fever* presents a family where deeply religious, apparently middle-class parents have one son who is a successful architect and another who is the most dismal example of the underclass: a thieving, conniving, crack cocaine abuser. *Jungle Fever*, while ostensibly about heterosexual relations between African and Euro-Americans, takes on the issues of drug abuse within the African American community with a vengeance. Unlike *Do the Right Thing*, about which critics complained that Lee showed a drug-free inner-city Black community, or *She's Gotta Have It*, which alluded only casually to Mars Blackmon's underclass status, there is no doubt that the *Jungle Fever* character Gator Purify, despite having been "raised right" by discipline-conscious, loving parents, has fallen and become a drug addict, whereas his younger brother, Flipper, has attained the American dream. *Jungle Fever* shows undisciplined Blacks, whites, and Latinos at their worst, selling drugs or drawn to the "Taj Mahal," a place where drug abuse seems to be a twenty-four-hour-a-day occupation for hundreds of people.

As displayed in *Jungle Fever*, the plight of the underclass is not an individual phenomenon. Unfortunately, again, Lee fails to present his viewers with a clear idea of why or how this underclass behavior came about. Is Gator, despite having been "raised right," a drug addict because his father was too overbearing and mother too lenient? If so, is a dysfunctional family life also the reason hundreds of others flock to the Taj Mahal? Or has Gator—like those hundreds of others—been unable to find a job paying a living wage? Outside the Taj Mahal, Flipper, a neighborhood boy, is nearly accosted by an apparent childhood friend, now a drug dealer, as he searches for his drug-crazed brother. Young girls approach Flipper on the street offering to perform oral sex in exchange for money to buy drugs. Drug addiction is of epidemic proportions in *Jungle Fever*, yet Spike Lee never says why this is the case. Worse than this, however, he portrays only one solution.

Ossie Davis, Wesley Snipes, Annabella Sciorra, and Ruby Dee
in *Jungle Fever* (Cineaste/David Lee)

If a drug abuse program is a viable option, it is not offered by Lee. Rather, Flipper's father, a preacher and a doctor according to the script, is left with no option but to shoot his eldest son, Gator— killing him rather than minister to his drug addiction. Perhaps Lee is convinced that his viewers will be so appalled at this solution they will seek some other. But since the release of *Jungle Fever*, two African American mothers in New York have shot and killed their drug-addicted daughters. If they attended Spike Lee films for counsel in this matter, they have followed his counsel to the letter. Death—by the closest kin—is the only solution *Jungle Fever* offers those of the Black urban underclass.

Criticism versus Complicity

While the underclass continues to exist, however, the media has an additional role to play. Although neither capitalists nor taxpayers wish to take on the financial burden of eliminating the underclass, someone must, while it exists, encourage the overall underclass population to remain loyal to the State, pay taxes, avoid crime, and not riot as protest against their unfortunate condition. The media actually takes on the role of church, school, and family in broadcasting the message of self-discipline to inner-city populations. In some cases it must disguise or hide problems: for example, keep the public ignorant of judicial decisions until the police can be put in place, to maintain order, as in the second Rodney King–related police trial in Los Angeles.

Average Americans, capitalists, and the underclass demand, and will pay for, explanations of and potential solutions to the underclass condition. To avert crises in general, then, and to make a profit, the media find and reward persons seen as legitimate by the underclass (and other interested parties) who will comply with and assist in attempts to manufacture and disseminate almost any superficial description of or solution to the problems of the underclass. The more exciting, thrilling, or convincing the player, the more popular he or she becomes, the more often the public will pay to hear his or her opinion. One of the most obvious people fulfilling this function, whether he likes it or not, is Spike Lee.

Despite the media's efforts to inculcate discipline, people of all races and classes commit crime. Yet most evident to white media consumers are youthful, Black, mostly male, poor people, whose arrests and alleged crimes receive disproportionate media attention. Such acts can be perceived as what Antonio Gramsci calls "quiet riots," that is, individual protests against negative treatment underclass members receive from the capitalist class and other taxpayers. Today, quiet rioters are locked up for a little while, then released to prey on, generally, under- and middle-class communities as well as on downtown shopping areas to which Blacks now have access as a result of desegregation. Thus quiet rioters are visible to white Americans, and such visibility stimulates both fear and curiosity in whites.

Neither Hollywood's distributors nor film producers, however, have a critical consciousness or nuanced social science education that encompasses the real causes of the underclass nor solutions to its problems. By his own account, for example, Spike Lee has a very limited social science background. In neither high school nor at university did Lee take social studies courses to augment his academic knowledge of African Americans, "Just literature," he said.[47]

Lee is not reluctant to emphasize his immersion in the world of music, literature, and art ever since his mother took him to musical performances and he attended his father's jazz performances before the age of ten.[48] Unlike his friend and fellow filmmaker Reginald Hudlin, who found inspiration in the War on Poverty–sponsored art programs for youth, Spike says that his mother, a high school art teacher, "ran an art program at home."[49] Art programs may teach one how to make films, but they generally limit their film critique to aesthetic and technical issues and ignore sociocultural and political concerns. Lee himself has been critical of this tendency and was less than happy in an NYU class that lauded the aesthetic and technical achievements of D. W. Griffith's *Birth of a Nation* but ignored the racism so clearly displayed in this film.

School Daze opens with photographs of intellectual activists such as Booker T. Washington and Marcus Garvey. Lee idolizes Malcolm X and Dr. Martin Luther King Jr. and places their words in his films. If his methodological adroitness extends backward to include a sociologist like W.E.B. Du Bois, should not his current-period research include contemporary Black social scientists?

Without a critical consciousness of the problem, Hollywood's attempt to assuage the public's fears and satisfy its curiosity, and the filmmakers' attempts to explain the problem, actually divert public attention from the real problem. This diversion puts off satisfaction of social ills and still further disenfranchises the underclass. Such actions reveal the filmmaker not as underclass advocate but, rather, in actual complicity in the maintenance or even exacerbation of inner-city poverty and powerlessness.

Spike Lee's complicity with the very systems he critiques is perhaps not different from that of most postmodern social critics. The paradox of postmodern critics, from a political standpoint, rests in their criticism of increasing wealth concentration and expansion of joblessness on the one hand, coupled with their patriotic support of the existing economic and social order on the other.

While being critical of those in dominant economic and political decision-making positions, the critics are "inextricably bound up with" those making and executing the decisions. Linda Hutcheon, author of *The Politics of Postmodernism*, says that "this is a strange kind of critique, one bound up, too, with its own *complicity* with power and domination, and one that acknowledges that it cannot escape implication in that which it nevertheless still wants to analyze and maybe even undermine."[50] This rather confused critique-while-dominating circularity is illustrated in veteran actor Ossie Davis's foreword to Spike Lee's book *The Construction of School Daze* and is part and parcel of the seeming contradiction between so-called independent filmmakers who never want to create a typical "Hollywood" movie but thirst and compete for Hollywood financing and distribution:

> Spike himself is independent, both in thought and action. He doesn't give much of a damn for Hollywood's opinion of himself or of his works. But he is perfectly willing to use Hollywood money—why not? Spike is first and foremost a damn good businessman, tough as nails! But that's about as close as he will allow Hollywood to come. Leave me the check, go home, and wait till I send for you. That's Spike's attitude, reminding me of Malcolm X a little.
>
> If Spike was indeed just a fluke, if he couldn't perform up to professional standards, if he wasted time and money, if he went down to Atlanta and fell on his ass, this would be held not only against him, but against the rest of us as well. That's what racism means.[51]

Theatrical film distribution companies, for example, attract large paying audiences by releasing depictions of underclass Blacks as principal figures in horror, adventure, and comedy films that reduce white fear of Blacks through invocation of traditional, nonthreatening stereotypes. Films with these formulaic elements, rather than films with primary elements such as Black romance, family drama, socioeconomic uplift, or historical biography, will seem more marketable to a mass audience by profit-oriented distributors.

Neither filmmakers, distributors, middle-class taxpayers, nor, in many cases, capitalists are necessarily consciously malicious in this activity. However, though holding fast to criticism of the dominating, negative impact American society has on the underclass, Spike Lee, like postmodernists, is complicit with this society in furthering the very domination he abhors.

This perfidious alliance between filmmakers and the "powers

that be," which Public Enemy's song "Fight the Power" so stridently condemns in *Do the Right Thing*, is manifest in precisely the artistic philosophy the new Black filmmakers espouse: individual choice and technical proficiency as their ultimate objective. In the many interviews I have conducted with Black filmmakers, very few believed they should be responsible to any group, person, or philosophy beyond their own moral and artistic selves. In response to the question of what kinds of scripts he thought young filmmakers should do, Lee demonstrated his concern that original writing and cinematic technical proficiency rather than social responsibility be fundamental concerns for emerging filmmakers:

> Me?? I'm just looking for original voices. I don't wanna read a script from a movie I've already seen ten million times now and it's only different cause it's Black now or you've put it in a hip-hop-world genre. I don't wanna read that shit. Another thing I think is lacking, I don't see any love of cinema. You look at *Boyz N the Hood*, you can tell John Singleton loves cinema. He's studied it, knows film history. I mean, a lot of these people have this Matty Rich approach: "I never picked up a camera before, I ain't go to no film school, I don't wanna go to film school, I don't wanna learn about film, I'm just making a movie." I mean, filmmaking is a craft. You gotta learn that shit. You gotta love cinema. I'm not saying you have to go to film school, but you gotta know something about film. Have some knowledge of the craft.[52]

Asked whether Black filmmakers should have "social responsibility," that is, think about what their films say or instruct people to do, award-winning documentarian and aspiring feature director Stanley Nelson responded:

> My own opinion on this? I don't think a filmmaker has any responsibility at all to the community. I don't think you can do that. It puts too much weight on you. Your responsibility is to yourself as an artist. You have a right to put shit up on the screen and people have a right not to go see it. . . . I mean, there are two distinct worlds of filmmaking, before *She's Gotta Have It* and after *She's Gotta Have It*. Imagine if Spike had sat down and said, "Am I being socially responsible to the Black community with this film!" . . . I don't think that as a filmmaker I can sit around and say, "Am I being socially correct?"[53]

(*Right to left*) Writer-producer-director Matty Rich co-stars in *Straight Out of Brooklyn* with Lawrence Gilliard Jr. and Mark Malone *(Cineaste)*

Such notions of social responsibility as divorced from the artistic may be seen as incongruent with Blacks' recent adoption of the group title "African American." While art production is defined as individualistic and isolated in European and American culture, it is not for the African. In fact, says Professor Talmadge Anderson, "the European term and concept of 'art' is not easily translatable into any of the various African cultures. . . . In the African tradition and frame of reference, objects, dance, music, and song were not perceived as art but as functional creations and symbols of life."[54]

Reginald Hudlin broadens the concept and gets to the heart of day-to-day reality in saying:

> In terms of literally what responsibilities do we have, well look, we live in a capitalistic society. We don't have responsibility for anybody to do anything, you know. We live in a sink or swim world. However, my personal opinion is that every human being has a responsibility to be a moral and good person and to be a good citizen to the world and to others. I don't care if you're a fireman, a janitor, or a filmmaker, you should do things that make the world a better place [rather] than a worse place. What I don't believe in as a filmmaker, I don't believe in being

a P[ublic] R[elations] person for Black people or for underclass people. Nor do I think we need one. I think that is based on [a false premise]: that the problem of racism is just that we don't understand each other. And if we did, things would be better. That's not true. There's a lot of misunderstanding, ignorance and stupidity but there are good economic reasons why those things continue. And if you really want to get rid of those problems you have to deal with the economic reasons why there is racial prejudice. I mean, you [whites] gotta have a group, like, that is considered inherently inferior so these other people can feel better, so they can get better jobs. I mean, there are all kinds of real, nuts and bolts reasons. I mean, all this holding hands . . . I'm not gonna say that doesn't provide some remedy, but it's not going to fundamentally address these problems.[55]

Although he is a brilliant film director and marketing genius, Lee's films do not explain the underlying economic structure of the racial domination they depict. The first step toward remedying the situation is a full explanation and articulation of this structure. In *Do the Right Thing*, for example, Spike Lee does not show the boarded-up factories all over Brooklyn in which Blacks once worked for high, union wages. He never explains why Mookie works in a low-paying pizza parlor rather than in a unionized factory.

Capitalist focus on nuclear weapons and runaway shops ruined the U.S. manufacturing base and led to huge trade imbalances with Japan and Germany. Americans buy VCRs and cars exported from abroad but manufacture high-tech weapons, which are mostly purchased by their own government. It is the contemporary absence of these factory jobs—not the presence of Sal's Pizzeria—that explains the underclass condition. This misreading of the situation leads to Lee's unfortunate replacement of symptoms of the problem—for example, acquisitive Koreans and Italians who take Blacks' rightful opportunities—for causes of the problem. What Lee indicates is that Black cultural pathology—moral decay and the demise of the Black family (single mothers and other parents do not discipline their kids)—not the operation of global politics and economics, is the underlying problem for inner-city Blacks.

Lee is complicitous with the capitalist class because this class does not care why or how underclasses exist, yet Lee helps it sell movie tickets and keep protests at a minimum by dispensing pseudo-solutions and pseudo-explanations of the underclass plight. Because Lee has not taken the time for significant study of the social sciences as they relate to this issue, his remains a tentative and attenuated view of the Black urban underclass that frustrates public understanding of the issues.

To solve the underclass problem, capitalists or taxpayers will have to provide jobs for the underclass rather than take advantage of cheap labor and other incentives abroad. They will also have to focus on consumer rather than military production so more American-produced goods are sold domestically and abroad. Lee never says these things, and unless he studies the issues he will never be able to raise mass consciousness of them.

Chapter 9 The Struggle Continues behind the Camera

The prerequisite for having a sustained career in the film industry for African American men and women is skills and education sufficient to make a valued contribution. However, large numbers of African Americans, even in Los Angeles and New York City where films are regularly made, while subjects now of numerous productions, are rarely paid members of the production team. Unemployment among African Americans remains—in good and bad economic times—far above the national average. Jaynes and Williams say:

> Changes in the labor market opportunities available to blacks are illustrated by the fact that the median earnings of $71,000 that black men born in 1914 could expect to earn over their lifetimes after age 25 had grown by a factor of 6 to $427,000 for black men born in 1959. Yet, while the relative expected earnings of black men had risen 15 percentage points, black men's expected median lifetime earnings were one-half that of white men of the same age cohort, a small improvement over 45 years.[1]

Joblessness among African Americans—black men, in particular—is the central cause of the black urban underclass. No single industry can be expected to solve African America's unemployment problems. But it seems reasonable that since Hollywood has so benefited from Black box office dollars, some return of dollars from this industry is justified. Eddie Murphy and Richard Pryor reigned as nearly the only broadly featured African American film actors in the late 1970s. The early 1980s saw a gradual increase in Blacks on the screen: Sidney Poitier produced and directed *Fast Forward*, and the team of George Jackson and Doug McHenry produced Michael

Director Michael Schultz on the set of *Krush Groove*
(Museum of Modern Art/Film Stills Archive)

Schultz's *Krush Groove* for Warner Bros., then *Tougher than Leather* for New Line Cinema. Finally, in 1986, Robert Townsend's *Hollywood Shuffle* and, in particular, Spike Lee's *She's Gotta Have It* "opened the floodgates" as Blacks were given contracts for work both behind and in front of the camera in up to twenty films theatrically released in a single year.

The increased distribution of films by African American filmmakers has been accompanied by an increased number of trained African Americans employed in the film industry. Some of these African American film workers are from the Black urban underclass. Although film industry jobs begin as intermittent employment, many workers become well respected and highly skilled over time. Excluding actors, film productions often employ 150 to 200 highly skilled persons for periods ranging from two weeks to over six months. In addition, work on a single film can so train and prove the worth of an individual worker that he or she may be invited to begin a career, and at a much elevated salary. Although no single industry can solve the underclass employment dilemma, is there a way for increased distribution of African American films to address the employment picture for African Americans?

Grace Blake, one of the very few Black female line producers in the Hollywood industry, makes no bones about the fact that race matters when it comes to hiring film crews. On her first film, *Lovers and Other Strangers*, to which she brought only secretarial skills, Blake worked as assistant to the production coordinator. "It was so exciting. It was the most exciting time of my life. It was fabulous, all these stars and stuff." Despite her excitement, however, Blake also remembers that it "was an all-white film. . . . I think actually there were two others [Black people on the crew], a grip and a prop guy . . . out of, oh gosh, a whole crew, which is usually over a hundred people."[2] Grace Blake presents an example of the opportunity available to a first-time crew person because her first, low-paying, behind-the-camera experience has led to a two-decade-long ascent up the Hollywood film production ladder. Although Blake works most often as a line producer, she has held positions of even greater control. Not only was she executive producer for Spike Lee's second feature, *School Daze* (1988), but she was also associate producer for the Oscar-winning *Silence of the Lambs* (1991).

> And you know something, [Blake says,] it has not changed. . . . If you go, right now, today, on any given set, you may find two or three Black people on the entire crew except of course, if it's a film about Black people, and even then, the technicians are all Caucasians because that's the way it is in this industry. I've worked a lot of films over the years and even on those films with producers and directors who are sensitive to the "Black cause" you may find ten [Blacks] in that particular crew. I mean, the percentage is really small . . . almost zero.

The line producer is the person who hires heads of individual film production departments such as lighting, camera, etc., so Blake has been very much, as filmmakers say, "in the mix" on the production employment scene. This very practical experience over a considerable length of time has conditioned her thoughts on the race/employment issue. "I used to knock Spike Lee," she said, "even though I worked with him on *School Daze*. Today I put him up on a pedestal" because he insists on having Blacks behind the camera.

Spike Lee's insistence on a high percentage of Blacks and other nonwhites on his film crews, while lauded among film technical personnel, is not new, however. As far back as Gordon Parks's 1969 film, *The Learning Tree*, Blacks in controlling positions, even in Hollywood-funded productions, have demanded increased nonwhite participation. Parks said with deserved pride:

> How can you help but say it's getting better when *The Learning Tree*, which was absolutely the first big black film made in Hollywood, was made on the Warner Bros. lot and was a $3 million production? I had fourteen or fifteen people behind the camera for the first time in the history of films. There was a black director. The producer was black. The scoring was done by a black man. The third cameraman for the first time was a black man. This was the first time in the history of motion pictures, and we did our thing. In *Shaft*, we've done the same thing. The gaffer [electrician] was black, the wardrobe mistress was black, the third assistant was black. Isaac Hayes did the music. Tom McIntosh, who is black, assisted him. We had two other black guys assisting him. I can name all down the line. There were black guys in just about every department. And I insisted on this, and MGM backed me up. I was a black American doing a black film in Hollywood. I don't have to tell you everybody was looking and saying, "Can he do it?" Hollywood was looking too. I was taking on the double thing of: Can a black and white crew mix? I was taking all those chances on my first picture that nobody ever took before.[3]

While Gordon Parks, Spike Lee, and other Blacks continue to demand that people of color be given jobs behind the camera, the overall Hollywood film industry is quite far from following suit.

Yet few would call more than 95 percent of all white film directors and producers racist because they do not hire Blacks. Rather, Blake says, "It's the same situation you have in schools . . . you have Black kids and white kids but when it comes time for lunch, the Black kids go and sit with the Black kids and the white kids, go and sit with the white kids. . . . It's a natural phenomenon." In addition to this "natural" or "unintentional" racial selection based on association, Blake mentions the film craft unions, of which she says:

> Even today . . . you work on a production and you find all of the people in a specific category all [blood] related, especially the

grips and the gaffers. . . . And it's a very closed business, its a closed shop. Nobody really wants to tell anybody anything. They don't want to teach anybody anything. And to me that's one of the ways we, as Black people, have been kept out of this business.

If nepotism and limited personal association across racial groups, as Blake has suggested, have constrained African American entree into technical film production employment, how might these constraints be reduced and film employment more fully serve to alleviate the plight of the urban underclass?

Youth-oriented art programs, some a part of the Great Society and War on Poverty youth programs of Lyndon Johnson's administration, have for more than thirty years introduced inner-city children to a broad range of career paths. Reginald Hudlin, Harvard graduate and writer/director of multimillion-dollar feature films *House Party* and *Boomerang*, tells many stories of his and his brother Warrington's youthful experiences in the East St. Louis government-sponsored art programs.

It's really, literally, about jobs, and creating opportunities. I mean, besides my parents [his mother has a Ph.D., his father has a master's], the other thing that was incredible in East St. Louis, that made a difference for a lot of people, was Katherine Dunham's programs. She came to East St. Louis because it was in such a state of poverty and disrepair. And she really made all those Great Society programs work. . . . She had master drummers from Senegal, people like Shelby Steele and Henry Dumas teaching college prep courses to high school kids. She had Yoruba language classes and dressmaking. She brought martial arts from Asia and Brazil. The free lunch program was there so people could get something to eat.

Reginald says he remembers those programs very well, even though at the time he "wore a size zero karate gi [uniform]."

Personal testimony, personal income tax records, and demonstrated private and public sector accomplishment indicate that Great Society and similar youth programs worked while they lasted. For example, Reginald Hudlin offers some significant memories: "There was a guy, I think Bradox was his name. Everyone says he was a hood. He was a bad man. But there he is [today], a serious dancer. I mean serious about it. [Dunham] just inspired a lot of people [and] opened the world up to a lot of people." Reginald recalls a particularly poignant incident at the Dunham program's lunch room:

> There was a Black motorcycle guy, and he had his jacket covered with studs and drawings, and the whole nine [yards], and he had a big helmet on and he had it covered with animal fur and the horns coming out of it. And he was very super-ornate. Then this African brother walked in wearing this African print covered with cowrie shells. And they saw each other and it was the entire diaspora right there, because they were identically dressed! One brother did it with studs, the other brother did it with cowrie shells, but clearly, they had the exact same aesthetic, working in different materials an ocean apart. They circled each other and grinned. And the whole room grinned, because it was right there. And what was incredible was not just that they were brought together, but that there were courses there that made us understand exactly what [we] were seeing. It wasn't a mere coincidence.[4]

Reginald also recalls the frustration he felt at his high school buddies' refusal, even at his own urging, to apply to Ivy League schools. "They just assumed they wouldn't get in," he said. Reginald, however, had accomplished parents and antipoverty programs to push him forward. He also had his older brother, Warrington, who had graduated with honors from Yale University. Yet Warrington's Yale admission had only come after his attendance at the 1969 session of the short-lived Yale Summer High School program for disadvantaged youth.[5]

The accomplishments of Spike Lee, who attended no Great Society programs because, he says, "my mother ran an arts program in her basement," demonstrate that African American children of educated parents, without government sponsorship, can attain the American dream.[6] Yet, while the children of middle-class or educated parents can benefit from participation, such programs are designed to reduce the numbers of people in the underclass.

Cliff Frazier's twenty-year tenure as an antipoverty film program administrator offers some indication of the potential for success among the least advantaged. Frazier says:

Cliff Frazier (*center*) directs a scene for the Community Film
Workshop of the 1970s *(Cliff Frazier)*

When the AFI [American Film Institute] created the Community Film Workshop Council [CFWC, in response to an impas-
sioned speech by AFI board member Sidney Poitier] we were
able to get money from the Office of Economic Opportunity
(OEO) to set up two projects: (1) to set up TV and film workshops around the country and (2) to train broadcast journalists.
So we set up workshops in Hartford, Connecticut, Santa Fe,
Chicago, Los Angeles, San Francisco, Whitesburgh, Kentucky,
New York. . . . We set up these workshops as a tool to bring
groups together where there was alienation. In Whitesburgh,
Kentucky, you had the coal miners, the workers, and the youth
all polarized. Our intent was to take the technology and teach
the local people to use the technology so they could articulate
through media, through film or TV, their perspectives. Their attitudes. And to use this existing product to bring people together to talk about, to analyze, and to express, again, another
perspective. And as you begin to have this visual dialogue, you
begin to find areas of commonality, areas in which people can
come together.[7]

The Whitesburgh workshop currently exists as Appalachia's nationally famous Appalshop television and film program devoted to

an almost totally Euro-American, poverty population. Frazier goes on to indicate the degree of regional hostility.

> When we first set up the workshop in Appalachia we were bombed out. They didn't want us there. And by the way, the director of that program [Yale architect and filmmaker Bill Richardson] was a white cat. He was from that area, only he was from Ohio, close to the Appalachians. . . . So he was bombed out, burned out, so he went to another location. And this time, rather than try to get the people involved, he just got the place and set up the equipment, put his chair on the porch, and sat back and relaxed. And the people walking by, seeing the equipment, became interested, because he had a monitor set up on the porch [and] they could see themselves. That gradually began to get them interested and so they came in on their own. He didn't go to them. Over a period of time Appalshop became the most phenomenal production facility in the Appalachian region. They had a record company. They have a radio station. They had a theater. And they're still doing film and TV production. In fact, one of the former students became executive director of the Kentucky Arts Commission.

In yet another example, the Santa Fe, New Mexico, Community Film Workshop was run by and focused on the local population of Native American youths. George Burdeau, the program's director and a Native American, was hired fresh out of film school. He ran the program "until the money ran out," then pursued a successful career as a director in public broadcasting.

The Dunham program in East St. Louis, Cliff Frazier's various programs all over the United States, and other, similar programs were financed by governmental and philanthropic sources. They flowered in the 1960s and 1970s and were generally dead in the 1980s. Continuation of them might have provided a bridge between the inner city and the film industry. Instead, by the 1990s, some poor Blacks no longer waited for NAACP leadership to demand more jobs.

Reports of conflicts over behind-the-camera employment have increased since 1990. For example, in a front-page October 1991 article entitled "Blacks See Red over Lily-white Film Crews," *Variety*'s Michael Fleming wrote that "Hollywood may have opened its doors to Black directors, but film crews still have the racial mix of a professional hockey team." *Variety* reported that two days before shooting ended on the New York set of *Used People* in 1991, "a group of black activists burst [in] and threatened to shut down filming until the producers agreed to hire two blacks as entry-level production assistants." The "Black activists" were headed by Mustafa Majeed of the Communications Industry Skills Center (CISC), which has created a directory of minority technical personnel for use by film industry producers. The group's city-government funding was cut in the summer of 1991 as a result of another New York fiscal crisis. While CISC compiles a list of potential employees and presents persons to take jobs, it apparently has no reliable means either to screen employment seekers or to augment their skills. A reading of *Variety*'s report on the two African Americans hired on *Used People* indicates that they may have been from the truly disadvantaged group of which Wilson speaks:

> Sources say the producers of "Used People" agreed to hire two black p.a.'s in unskilled positions after the "visit" to the set by Majeed. Only one showed up the next morning, say sources, and stayed just three hours before telling the producer he had to leave to visit his parole officer. Though he was told he could work the rest of his hours in the evening and still get paid, he didn't show again—until the next day, demanding a paycheck.[8]

Strong-arm tactics, however, are unlikely to provide a solid foundation for continued, long-term employment of African Americans within the film industry, although they have stimulated the New York City film community to action regarding the employment of nonwhites. *Variety* reported on March 2, 1992, in an article entitled "NY Panel Offers Plan to Integrate Crews," that "in response to increasing pressure for racial integration of crews, the New York film community [pitched] studios on a plan that would create 23 trainee positions for minorities on Gotham locations." This Film Industry Leg-Up for Minorities program was to be open only to nonwhites. It was constructed by the newly created Committee for Positive Action (CFPA), chaired by Hollywood feature film director Sidney Lumet and including as members Grace Blake, "IA rep Brian Unger, IA Local 644 president Doug Hart, IA Local 52 president Frank Schultz, Bronx Community College president Roscoe Brown, city and state film commissioners Jaynne Keys and Pepper O'Brien, and production managers and producers like G. Mae Brown, Preston Holmes (who works with Spike Lee), David Picker, and Tribeca Productions' Jane Rosenthal." The major goal of this program was to get nonwhites into the film unions. According to Amy Sultan, plan coordinator and city assistant director of film: "The idea is that most continued employment in film is based on working relationships, not resumes. Starting a mentor program to create relationships is the closest thing to replicating the traditional family relationships in the unions." Later in the same article, however, Sultan seems at first enthusiastic, then contradictory, and finally pessimistic about the plan's chances for success. She says that funding for the program will be sought from the studios. If they do not endorse the plan, however, she is confident it will happen one way or another:

> It's not contingent on the studios, but they can make it happen faster. We can scale down the program if we can't get that kind of funding.
> But without the studio funding there really is no point. Without their commitment to change, one can't expect the unions to do it alone. It has to be a joint effort, and this in itself is a modest effort to bring about change. It isn't in itself a solution.[9]

The estimated total cost of the twenty-six-week-long program was $500,000. But private funding turned out to be very hard to come by. The mentor program remains, at this writing, a plan ready to be put into action without the money to make it a reality. In spring 1995, the committee had intended to work with Bill Cosby Productions to expand minority film participation; however, a cut in Cosby's shooting schedule caused cancellation of the program. A meeting to determine the committee's course of action for the future was planned for the fall.[10]

The task of getting African Americans behind the camera on white-controlled films remains arduous. *Variety* reports that the demand for Blacks behind the camera "changes only when films steered by black Helmers come to town, when the percentage of blacks in crews rises from 1 percent to 5 percent to as much as 80 percent."[11] Of course, no one expects the film industry to be the employment engine for all of African America. If we consider that an average crew size is one hundred persons, that prior to 1985 the number of African American films produced and distributed averaged fewer than two per year, and that since 1985 the average yearly number of African American films has been six per year, the employment impact of more African American films is worthy of consideration: averaging 160 jobs per year before 1985 and 480 per year after 1985. By contrast, on the four hundred non-Black films, by *Variety*'s calculation, only four hundred behind-the-camera jobs are held by African Americans. Job creation alone, then, seems justification for governmental attention to increasing the number of African American film productions. According to Cliff Frazier, many who work on African American films are from disadvantaged, inner-city backgrounds. But as working people they pay taxes, are unlikely to commit crimes, and are not a drain on the U.S. welfare systems.

Construction of a high-percentage African American film crew is not a simple matter, however. Reginald Hudlin says that while he is a strong supporter of affirmative action in hiring decisions, a problem in building a skilled Black crew is that such people are in high demand within the industry: Blacks who have "made it" have had to work so hard, they are three times more skilled and often better educated than their white counterparts. Individual skilled Blacks, therefore, from a purely merit-based vantage point, receive many, many more job offers than do individual whites.[12] The African American location sound person on *Boomerang*, for example, had two Oscar awards already on his shelf. These skilled African Americans are the exceptions to the rule, however. The average Black man or woman seeking film employment brings no skills and a lifetime of negative social and psychological baggage to the set.

Grace Blake, line producer on *Boomerang*, says that Warrington Hudlin demanded and received from the film's distributor, Paramount Pictures, $50,000 to hire ten to twelve interns who had never before been on a shoot. This brought the nonwhite percentage of the crew to about 60 percent.

> I was the person who helped the young people [Blake says]. I basically did it on my own, because having the experience and seeing what [the Hudlin brothers] were trying to do, [I knew

that] you can't do it for a friend. . . . You have to interview each person and make sure this is what they really want to do. I'm not going to waste my time with "your friend" when it's obvious that person is just there for the glamor of it. You're either coming to work or I don't have the time for you. . . . Some of the people [who] came out of that program have gone on to do very well [even though employed] just during *Boomerang*. I mean, I know one who has not stopped working since [and is getting paid for it].

Of Spike Lee's efforts Blake says:

I used to fault him for being too agressive, for wanting it too quickly. While he was giving a lot of the young people a chance to work on a production, a lot of them didn't have the experience. They didn't belong to the unions. . . . I think he's beginning to realize . . . he's kind of evened off a little bit. Understanding, having spent the past six or seven years doing production after production after production, [he is realizing] that you have to be in it. . . . You can't be a separate entity. It's one big Hollywood situation. . . . I think most movies will come out of Hollywood or you'll become isolated. . . . There is no such thing as a nonunion movie anymore.

Spike Lee's 1994 film, *Crooklyn*, was a union shoot with very few nonunion employees. As Hollywood studios, mini-majors (such as New Line), and boutique distributors attached to bigger firms (such as IRS, Miramax, or Gramercy) finance and distribute an increasing percentage of Black films, it is increasingly probable that African American film workers will have to bring skills and a union card the first day on the set.

Of all the film industry employment intervention methods—strong-arm tactics, studio-funded union apprenticeships, film internships demanded by individual Blacks in positions of control on individual shoots, and government and/or philanthropic sponsorship of training programs—the last seems best suited to address the broad underemployment conditions Wilson credits most for the continuation of an underclass. Negotiation on a per film basis, a current characteristic of all tactics listed except this one, is unmanageable and unrealistic because in film locations where few nonwhites live, unless someone in a position of control makes an extra effort, it is unlikely that nonwhites will be put on the crew; they are unlikely to be in unions, or if they are in unions they are likely to be in high demand; and they are unlikely to have personal or nepotistic associations with those hiring. However, because a high percentage of those in film craft unions are not college educated (a well-documented characteristic said to limit the opportunities of those in the underclass), film training programs designed to prepare trainees for union membership, particularly ones that include on-the-job training and apprenticeships (normal characteristics of film craft education), are unlikely to be demanding beyond the academic abilities of those in the underclass.

In 1965, Cliff Frazier was East Coast director of a program funded by the Brooks Foundation of Santa Barbara, California, to "put film technology in the hands of local people, African American people." Brooks responded to increasing "ghetto" unrest and, in particular, to the Watts revolt of that same year by funding the Mafundi Institute in Watts, Mobilization for Youth on New York City's Lower East Side, and a film program for Philadelphia's "12th and Oxford Street gang."

In Philadelphia at that time, Frazier says, even as their communities marched for civil rights,

> the gangs were regularly killing each other. Out of [the Brooks program], not only did they learn the technology, but the 12th and Oxford Street [gang], they set up their own businesses. They had a laundromat and they set up a film company and worked with Sidney Poitier on a film he was shooting there. . . . All [three programs] were successful at the time, but the problem is we did not have the resources to sustain it. Remember we were dealing with teenagers, to start them is one thing, but they need to be shepherded through. . . . We showed them how to use the technology. We showed them how to go into business. What would have worked better for them and for us is if we had had enough money to sustain it for three years. . . . [Brooks's funding] was for "the project." For making "the" film.

Frazier says that the Brooks Foundation "was discontinued. It was created by a rich, young white cat, and when he went on to other things it disappeared." Under the Nixon and/or Reagan administrations, however, federal funding was withdrawn from OEO and similar programs, Frazier says, on the assumption that private foundations and philanthropic organizations would take on the burden of urban intervention funding. The Brooks Foundation's having "gone on to something else" demonstrates clearly what folly this assumption was then and remains today. Philanthropy cannot be mandated as can government commitment and is therefore more fickle and undependable for solving entrenched, long-existent social ills.

Nineteen eighty-three marked the end of New York City's Institute for New Cinema Artists (INCA), Frazier's last attempt at inner-city training for media technicians. Frazier is currently creating the International Communications Association (ICA), a merger of three entertainment industry training and employment programs: Community Film Workshop Council (CFWC), Third World Cinema (TWC), and INCA. ICA's goal will be to retard degeneration of inner-city communities. Over twenty years these three programs have successively attempted to solve these social ills. But the major reason why they are three programs, rather than one long-lasting program, is the fickle, transient, unpredictable, and, currently, nonexistent nature of their funding. With ICA, however, Frazier intends to borrow a page from Spike Lee's book in the hope of overcoming funding indeterminacy.

Future Directions, the conference publication of ICA's 1992 "Reunion 2000," notes with pride that from 1968 the three member organizations "placed over 1500 minorities, women and others from disadvantaged communities into the media industries (motion picture, TV, recording and allied media) as directors, writers, producers, broadcast journalists, technicians and management personnel through the United States and abroad." Of program enrollees, this publication states that many "were alienated and misdirected individuals who found direction and forever changed their negative behavior into positive endeavor." In 1971, two program graduates working for WGR-TV in Buffalo, New York, "were the only broadcast journalists allowed in Attica Prison during the riot." In the same year, CFWC trained and placed America's first Black news-camerawoman at WMAL-TV in Washington, D.C. In addition, Preston Holmes, Spike Lee's line producer, documentarian Stanley

Preston Holmes, producer of Mario Van Peebles's *Panther*, slates the 1972 ABC-TV special *Turkey Treasure* as a student in Community Film Workshop, while the film's screenwriter, Fred Foster, sits in *(Cliff Frazier)*

Nelson, music video producer Deborah Bolling, Warrington Hudlin, and film and television director Neema Barnette are all ICA program graduates. Drake Walker, an apprentice on *Angel Levine*, the first movie on which CFWC students worked, went on to write the 1972 Sidney Poitier–Harry Belafonte film *Buck and the Preacher*. This was the first film to show postbellum Blacks responding in kind to violent white gangs trying to end their migration west and force their return to lives picking cotton in Louisiana.

ICA is charged to "develop initiatives that are aimed at reaching and motivating young people who have fallen into the abyss of criminal activity, alienation and general hostility."[13] This seems very much to be the population Wilson calls the truly disadvantaged.

"Oprah, Cosby," Frazier says, "might have two or three interns" in their operations. But "individuals do individual things." In order to train and place fifteen hundred disadvantaged people in a short time, a "structured, organized process was needed. It won't just happen out of the good wishes of someone." The ICA programs were multifaceted in that they not only trained people for more than one industry but also analyzed the entertainment industry to determine where jobs would be in the future and provided suitable training for emerging technologies such as cable and satellite television.

While a program like that outlined in ICA is consistent with presidential espoused desire to aid inner-city development and would be a good candidate for government funding, Cliff Frazier hopes to follow the path now being laid by Spike Lee. While ICA itself will be a nonprofit organization, it will spawn profit-making companies that focus on producing low-budget, commercial feature films for theatrical release. ICA will also create retail outlets for its products and, perhaps, other commercial ventures—a record or music company, for example, to mimic the ones Spike Lee has created. With Spike Lee's financial success, Cliff Frazier realized that creating profit-making institutions, rather than continuing to depend on funding sources as CFWC, INCA, and TWC had done in the past, was the way to build both independence and staying power at the service of the truly disadvantaged.

Conclusion

In 1986, the creative, entrepreneurial, and ideopolitical boldness of Spike Lee ushered in a new era of increased African American male control on individual, feature-length, commercially released motion pictures. By mid-1995, while some new Black filmmakers had accumulated three or more theatrical releases, Lee had seven of his own and two that he executive produced. He had also expanded his holdings in retail sales and music production. Between 1986 and 1995, significantly more African American–directed films were released than in the previous decade and a half.

This Spike Lee–initiated entrepreneurial flowering was perceived by many as long overdue. And, given American pretensions of individual liberty inscribed in the Declaration of Independence, the Bill of Rights, the Constitution, and numerous other laws, private corporate rules, and official proclamations, this seems a responsible view. The severity of post–civil rights struggles to carve a niche in corporate America for African American business and employment has been unexpected. Many new Black filmmakers, for example, expressed wonder that the Black Power period yielded mostly blaxploitation films, from which whites reaped the greatest benefit, rather than more firmly entrenched African American production and distribution companies.

In this continuing struggle, African Americans have had few dependable allies. Even financially successful Jews, white people vilified and oppressed—as Blacks have been—for centuries by both Arabs and Caucasians, proved equivocal. Universal's Carl Laemmle and the NAACP's Joel Spingarn exemplify this ambivalence.

In the 1910s, Universal, the most powerful film company of the day, forced Black superstar Noble Johnson to abandon his own fledgling Lincoln Motion Picture Company rather than share his box office allure. Laemmle was also more benevolent to his wealthy Jewish competitor, Thomas Ince, than to Booker T. Washington's struggling brethren. When Ince's company burned down, Lammele provided him an open line of credit, but he forced the Blacks to come up with $60,000 to produce a film countering the overt racism of D. W. Griffiths's *Birth of a Nation.*

Spingarn, an NAACP leader and true supporter of rights for African Americans, withdrew support when W.E.B. Du Bois sought Black development separate from, rather than integrated with, the dominant white economy. Since the beginning of the civil rights period, the NAACP, now with an African American leadership, has worked overtime filing lawsuits and threatening boycotts to force the Hollywood studios to hire more Blacks both in front of and behind the camera. The Screen Actors Guild, the Directors Guild of America, the U.S. government, and other organizations and individuals have joined this effort. However, it was not until the success and vocalized determination of Spike Lee to hire Blacks for technical positions and to write salutary roles for Blacks in films on which he held nearly total production and substantial marketing and distribution control that films authentically reflecting an African American worldview began to emerge.

While Spike Lee is rightfully called a phenomenon, it was not his talents alone that ushered in the change. Lee, in fact, was himself the product of political and economic forces far beyond his control. The Paramount Consent Decree of 1948, the invention of television, the post-1960s flowering of film schools, the majors' preoccupation with blockbusters, and the multiplexing of exhibition are industry-specific forces that favored independent producers like Spike Lee and Wayne Wang. Yet the American government's need to change post–World War II domestic racial policy is the force that massaged white America and made its acceptance of Spike Lee's racial brashness possible. It is these changing structural relationships that Lee and other individuals have taken advantage of to build their own fortunes.

Ironically, however, this building process has been internally contradictory. Lee's very success is founded on his opposition to the financial structures that undergird that success. In great part, this is the paradox of the talented social critic in postmodern times: the resources needed and acquired to protest "the system"—what Public Enemy called "the powers that be"—are provided by those powers and "the system" itself.

This situation renders the critic complicitous—that is, a partner with those "powers"—in maintaining the very structural relations he or she riles against. Thus the independence from Hollywood control so sought by auteurs and politically conscious artists is chimerical when funded by those very established Hollywood companies—Universal and Warner Bros. for Spike Lee.

Complicity has an even more insidious aspect, however, when viewed in a contemporary social science context. The new Black filmmakers may unintentionally help maintain the very social relationships and conditions their films protest. Spike Lee is an outspoken proponent of African American "uplift." He condemns Reagan-Bush socioeconomic policy for creating the deplorable urban condition codified as the Black urban underclass. Yet, beyond an amorphous cry of "racism," Lee's filmed and spoken social critiques provide explanations for neither the causes of the underclass condition nor the way in which macro-level social and economic policy actually operates; nor does he offer feasible solutions to the underclass problem. In fact, the only solution Lee offers is that course taken by two African American mothers in New York City: the "mercy killing" of their own drug-addicted children.

Although Lee's central characters may be underclass members—for example, Mars Blackmon and Mookie—Lee never explains why these men are unemployed or underemployed for years on end. Lee never talks about the fact that Blacks—Mars's and Mookie's relatives included—migrated north in large numbers because northern factories provided them well-paying union jobs in the 1940s and 1950s. Although he acknowledged in an interview that factories such as Wonder Bread are leaving the inner cities, he never shows that the jobs that had undergirded inner-city cultural and socioeconomic viability were taken to the suburbs where whites had fled or were sent abroad in search of cheap labor. The search for cheap labor is a global economic phenomenon that has had devastating effect on people with limited education and skills who remain in the inner cities after manufacturers have left. Lee never shows that such forces have a disproportionate negative impact that results in "ghetto" jobless-ness more than twice the rate in white areas. Such joblessness is now the foundation for crime, familial, and economic dissolution among the Black urban underclass.

Historic and contemporary racism undergirds the Black urban underclass. But the responsible social critic—artist or no—must show *how* this is accomplished. What are its mechanisms? How can it be attacked and dismantled? Research of the social, economic, and political context in which filmed characters live is necessary to pro-vide a complete picture. An example of the research neglected can be demonstrated by viewing the film *Malcolm X*. In response to the question "What sort of research did you do for the film?" Lee said:

> I read everything that I could, including a new book by Zak Kondo about the assassination that was very important in help-ing us re-create the assassination in the film. Paul Lee was a great help because he's someone who's really devoted his life to Malcolm X. Paul, who lives in Detroit, was in the Nation, I think, when he was twelve years old. As far as scholars go, I don't think there's anyone who knows more about Malcolm X than Paul Lee.
>
> I also talked to a lot of people, including Benjamin Karim, who's Benjamin 2X in the film, Malcolm's brothers—Wilfred, Omar Azziz, and Robert—his sister Yvonne, Malcolm's widow, Betty Shabazz, and Malcolm Jarvis, who's Shorty in the film. I also went to Chicago and talked to Minister Farrakhan. That's where a lot of the good stuff came from, going around the coun-try and talking to people who knew Malcolm. Not just his rela-tives, but people who were in the Nation with him, in the OAAU, and so on.[1]

The research design outlined by Lee is clearly focused on Malcolm X as an individual, not as an actor within a given socioeco-nomic and political context. This research design is a major failing in the film's ability to faithfully reproduce the environment that nur-tured Malcolm X. It appears that the personality and charisma Malcolm evinced were more important to Lee than Malcolm's im-pact on African America's social reality.

Dr. Todd Boyd, currently the only African American professor in the University of Southern California's film program, says, "Spike

Lee's *Malcolm X* suffers from a common tendency to recycle history into pure spectacle empty of meaningful political or intellectual content." Boyd says Lee fell into the trap of forcing Malcolm X into the American capitalist icon of the self-made man.

> Despite the ostensibly militant trappings of Malcolm's newfound theology, the film clearly embraces some of the most potent myths of American culture. Malcolm's ability to "pull himself up by his own bootstraps" fits neatly into the ideology of upward mobility, and, paradoxically, Malcolm emerges as more "American" than the elite Kennedys or the middle class, well-educated Martin Luther King, Jr.

Boyd also voices the concern that Lee ignores the sociopolitical context of Malcolm X's day. Malcolm is constructed in the film as if his goals were the pro-American humanism evinced by Lee himself and basketball players, such as Michael Jordan, who are current American cultural icons: "Lee refuses to address Malcolm's transformation from an archetypal 'race man' to an internationalist and pan-Africanist. The film merely honors Malcolm as a humanist, and this incomplete portrait of a complex man sets the stage for his enshrinement as a true "American."[2]

The director of Columbia University's African American Studies Program, Dr. Manning Marable, also emphasizes the ineffectiveness of Lee's research design.

> The ideological limitations of both [Alex] Haley and Lee keep their interpretations of Malcolm located on safe, religious grounds rather than on the more dangerous terrain of race and class struggle. . . . Both Lee and Haley ignore the long history of African-American nationalism in the U.S., preferring to see Malcolm as a "reaction" to white racism and prejudice, rather that as the product of a long and rich protest tradition.
>
> To really honor Malcolm X is to extend his political and ideological search into struggles of inequality, racism, and economic oppression which define Black liberation today. . . . The filmmaker's goal was to create a cultural icon, but the Black community does not need myths. It desperately requires practical solutions to its pressing problems.[3]

Spike Lee, many other African American filmmakers, and their critics eschew social scientific research in favor of a focus on aesthetics and emotional response to socioeconomic problems. Rarely do they evince a critical consciousness useful in explaining or solving the urban underclass problem. Instead, the aesthetics and emotion on screen serve to give both white and nonwhite audiences stimulating, attractive, but phony information in exchange for box office dollars. These revenues are shared by filmmakers and their financial backers, who are frequently distributors. "Hollywood," "the media," and associated upwardly mobile individuals may benefit financially and career-wise, but the Black urban underclass, as a class, is rarely aided by this exchange.

Two positive outcomes of continued success for new Black filmmakers would be extension of entree to African American women directors and increased employment for Blacks behind the camera. Line producers, the people who hire film crews, stipulate that having African Americans in controlling positions has a significantly greater impact on individual project employment of Blacks than does project control by whites. Despite the fact that Black women now hold positions as producers, line producers, and script supervisors and sometimes have been successful television directors, such behind-the-scenes work has not proved a conduit to the film director's chair. Various reasons are suggested for the continued paucity of African American women's stories and directorships, but the most persuasive reason is fear within the distribution arena.

The most consistently successful new Black films in terms of profit ratio have been in the ghetto/shoot-em-up genre—*Boyz N the Hood* being the best example. Black women, however, have been reluctant to produce in this male-dominated genre. Women express a preference for producing "feeling" films that focus on female bonding. *Daughters of the Dust* exemplifies this film type. This film was not picked up by a major studio, however, and did not gross more than double its negative costs, a profit ratio of two to one. *Boyz*, by contrast, produced a profit ratio of eight to one and laid the groundwork for distributors' current focus on genre.

In 1992, Miramax, now a part of Disney, picked up Leslie Harris's *Just Another Girl on the IRT*, despite the film's low production values. *IRT* is considered a "girlz n the 'hood"–type film, and a well-respected distributor received accolades for handling it.

Harris received the Independent Feature Project's 1993 Open Palm Award at the same Gotham Awards where the lifetime Achievement Award went to Martin Scorsese. Yet, despite *Daughters*'s general critical success, its director, Julie Dash, leaves profit-hungry distributors cold and fearful. Four years after *Daughters*'s release, Dash has yet to find funding for a second commercial production.

African American women's poor reception in financing circles is indicative of distribution's power to influence or determine film content prior to production. No matter the artistry of the director and the crew, if distributors do not expect to make money, they will not pay for the prints (copies of the film viewed in theaters are about $1,000 each); nor will they finance advertising or promotion; nor will they arrange showings through their extensive contacts with exhibitors. Market-wise writers and directors know this and create with product marketability in mind.

While most people directing in either the Hollywood or independent film industries are adequate in terms of both skill and artistic talent, only the spark of an exceptionally talented individual is capable of stimulating a revision in genre focus. From a distributor's standpoint the question is, where is the female version of Spike Lee?

In all probability she is now languishing in the bowels of the Black urban underclass. Giving this woman the skills and opportunity to break from the underclass existence is the objective of line producer Grace Blake and others in originating internship and educational programs aimed at aspiring nonwhite and female filmmakers. In November 1993, veteran actor Ossie Davis was keynote speaker for "Anatomy of an Industry," a conference designed to introduce members of the minority community to behind-the-camera careers. Grace Blake was moderator for this conference, which was sponsored by the Committee for Positive Action, "A Cooperative Venture of the State and City of New York Film Offices, Organized Labor and Concerned Industry Professionals." Conference panelists were Ann Carli, producer of *Blackout*, which became Darnell Martin's *I Like It Like That*; Bill Hanauer, business agent for Local 771, IATSE (the stage and film crew union); Terri Guarnieri, vice president of ABC Daytime Programming, East Coast; Preston Holmes, producer of

Barbara Tabokman, administrator, Local 161; Grace Blake; Gregory Hines; and Barbara Berger, business agent, Local 161, on the set of *Cotton Club* (*Grace Blake*)

Posse and some Spike Lee films; Rick Lopes, commercial director; Ina Mayhew, production designer; and Joe Trammell, president of Navesync Sound, Inc. Announcements of the conference were sent to New York City area high schools and colleges, particularly those serving nonwhite communities. Flyers advertised a roundtable discussion where representatives from many craft unions and film organizations spoke one-on-one with conference attendees about their professions and associations. Included were professionals representing a diverse cross-section of production careers, such as the arts (camera, editing, wardrobe, sound, hair and makeup, production design), business (accounting, production managers, law), and support services (props department, electrical, grip department).[4] The conference was held at Borough of Manhattan Community College, and the flyer provided specific bus and subway directions. The auditorium was filled to capacity with young people from all five New York boroughs and even from Newark, New Jersey. Some teenaged girls brought their mothers along.

The production of African American films should not be

neglected as a focus point for government- and industry-sponsored employment stimulation. The determination to put Americans back to work in the wake of the current recession would do well to note that moviemaking is an attractive career that does not require advanced education for either entree or success. Members of the Black urban underclass have demonstrated creative abilities in music production as well as in the graffiti found on municipal walls. They, and the white community, have also demonstrated a willingness to spend money to see African Americans on the screen. Because each film employs up to two hundred crew members and actors, increased support for low- and medium-budget feature productions, coupled with training programs based on the parameters of the "Anatomy of an Industry" conference outlined above, can have a significant impact on inner-city employment statistics and provide a respectable monetary and civic return on investment.

Epilogue

Since the late 1960s, when recently released Hollywood films were first broadcast on television, the marriage between these technologies has increased. For most of the last three decades, African American filmmakers have waged a struggle to become part of this Hollywood system. The economic and political realities integral to that battle are relevant to African American filmmakers now considering whether Hollywood remains the best, much less the exclusive, means to reach a mass audience. In any case, the structural environment that allowed a Spike Lee to emerge is collapsing, and with it the chance for other Black filmmakers to follow the course of Lee's early career. As always, the industry structure may be more important to most careers than artistic talent or lack thereof.

Vertical integration of distribution, production, and exhibition was against the law from 1948 until the Reagan years, when cable and VCRs became commonplace. As at the time of the studio system, there is now little room for independent distributors to make a buck. Exhibition is increasingly in suburban malls rather than central cities where Blacks are concentrated. In 1992, *Boxoffice* magazine reported there were twenty-three thousand theater screens in the United States. United Artists owned 2,357, Cineplex Odeon owned 1,618; American Multi-Cinema owned 1,589.[1] In 1994, only seven theaters in the entire United States were owned by African Americans.[2]

Film companies can even exhibit in our homes through their own television networks. Fox led the way, and now Paramount and Warner have introduced new television networks. With this level of major studio domination of all consumer markets, what need is there for Black producers with an independent point of view? In fact, the pattern of white director/Black cast is returning. *White Men Can't Jump*, *Who's the Man*, and *Fresh* are obvious examples. There is even the reappearance of benevolent colonialism in a white-directed film like *The Air Up There*, wherein a white male scouts basketball players in Africa.

Of course, a lot of blockbusters fail, as did *The Last Action Hero*, and the majors may want to continue to insure against such losses with inexpensive but very profitable African American productions. The profit ratios are spectacular. For every dollar invested in *Boyz N the Hood*, the first year's box office took in eight dollars. That's an eight-for-one return. The Hudlin brothers' *House Party* cost $2.5 million to make but grossed $26 million. That's a profit ratio of ten for one. Little wonder New Line has financed two sequels. The significance of these returns can be measured by comparing them to *Jurassic Park*, the all-time blockbuster big-budget movie. In its first year it returned five dollars for each dollar invested, quite good, but not near the ratio of the successful Black films. These ratios bode well for Black filmmakers, but there are problems. Black filmmakers who do not care if their films cross over to white audiences—for example, Julie Dash, director of *Daughters of the Dust*—are often less interested in dollars than in Black culture and politics. Such filmmakers are seen as ideologues rather than moneymakers and do not quite "fit" in a Hollywood cultural environment that focuses on, as former Columbia Pictures vice president Dennis Greene says, "glamorous projects" and "celebrity."[3] If executives can obviate these problems and still get sufficient audience attention to thwart competition by employing known white executives and directors, why not drop the inherent headache of potentially ideological Black control behind the camera?

Given these realities, a filmmaker who keeps his or her mind uniquely focused on theatrical release is almost doomed to failure. The future, as in the dawn of the sound era, is the new technology, areas where African Americans can carve out positions at an early stage of a new industrial structure.

There is plenty of room for African Americans in the expanding cable, direct-to-video, and CD-ROM/interactive video arenas. Electronics and telecommunications are already causing profound structural changes in the ways Hollywood does business. Soon movies will be transmitted to theaters by cable and satellite rather than by mail or messenger as they are now. Already pay-per-view cable and satellite television bring very recent releases into the home at half the single-admission theater cost in New York City. The advent of high-definition television is projected to narrow the viewing quality between theater and home screenings. Cable channels are making features solely for television release, bypassing theaters altogether. The Hudlin brothers are among the African Americans who have begun to explore this new structural period. Their *Cosmic Slop* (1994) on HBO featured three different Black directors and three different Black writers.

The mid-1990s saw the new Black filmmakers improve their craft and individual business positions, but the Hollywood industry did not see their numbers increase by very much. In fact, some of the directors who had released at least one film by 1992—for example, Julie Dash, Charles Lane (*Sidewalk Stories* [1989] and *True Identity* [1991]), and Leslie Harris—had yet to secure another project. David Johnson (*The Drop Squad* [1994] for Gramercy) and Preston Whitmore II (*The Walking Dead* [1995] for Savoy) were brought to their distributors by Black filmmakers, Spike Lee and the Doug McHenry/George Jackson team respectively. Neither of these films played well in either a Black or a crossover audience. *The Walking Dead*, billed as the Black man's experience of the Vietnam War, was condemned by Terrence Dixon of Rutgers University's *Observer* student paper. Dixon says he was moved when the white "captain put a gun to one of the [Black] soldier's mouth who was fresh out of high school" but was surprised and appalled by the "token Black comedian," whose humor seemed out of place. Dixon also said, with the exception of one female character, "the others were treated as if the writer hated women. There should have been a portrayal of the many strong and progressive African-American women struggling at [the] time when their men were contracted to possible death."[4]

Some of those already "in the mix," however, were doing substantial business volume. Doug McHenry added directing to his producing credits with *Jason's Lyric* in 1994. While criticized for casting a light-skinned actor as the hero and a dark-skinned actor as his despicably villainous brother, this film grossed nearly $30 million in less than one year. Spike Lee added directing and producing other

Rocky (Vondie Curtis-Hall, *center*) has an emotional discussion with the members of the "squad": (*left to right*) Stokeley (Eric A. Payne), Garvey (Ving Rhames), XB (Leonard Thomas), and Dwania Ali (Crystal Fox) in *Drop Squad* (*Gramercy Pictures*)

David Johnson, director and co-writer of *Drop Squad*
(*Gramercy Pictures*)

Producer George Jackson and producer-director Doug McHenry on the set
of *Jason's Lyric* (Gramercy Pictures)

Executive producer Spike Lee and director Nick Gomez on the set
of *New Jersey Drive* (Museum of Modern Art/Film Stills Archive)

Black Panther founders Bobby Seale (Courtney B. Vance)
and Huey Newton (Marcus Chong) keep watch in the
Mario Van Peebles film *Panther* *(Gramercy Pictures)*

people's works to his repertoire: his brother and sister co-wrote
Crooklyn, which Lee directed at the same time he was executive
producing both *The Drop Squad* and white director Nick Gomez's
New Jersey Drive. *Drive*, about Black carjackers in New Jersey, is the
first Lee work with a non-Black director.

Mario Van Peebles demonstrated strong directing and production credentials (along with his father, Melvin) on the set of *Panther*,
a 1995 Gramercy release. This film even received good reviews from
former members of the Black Panther Party, and at a prerelease
screening a majority Black audience in New York laughed, cheered,
and sighed in synch with the film's action.

John Singleton's *Higher Learning* (1994) dealt with conflicts ranging from white female sexuality to Black nationalists versus white skinheads in a way that caught people's attention and received mixed reviews. The bottom line, however, from the vantage point of the distributor, Columbia Pictures, is likely that it grossed over $30 million in fewer than six months.

Despite the fact that the majors have absorbed the larger independents, there is still a place for new distributors and for producers who refuse to adopt Hollywood formulaic dictates. New York's *Amsterdam News*, a Black-owned and -operated paper, deemed *Alma's Rainbow* "a film to love," and the *New York Times* called it a "promising directorial debut," but no distributor would handle it. The film is a coming-of-age story of a flamboyant aunt's influence on the relationship between a teen girl and her mother. Director Ayoka Chenzira self-distributed the $300,000 film to festivals and to limited theatrical release in Harlem, Brooklyn, and other locations.

Professor of journalism Bridgett Davis directly challenges the traditional Hollywood conception of women in the feature she wrote, produced, and directed, *Naked Acts*. Davis says that her sociopolitical message is not hidden. It is "layered and textured" throughout the film. The question posed is "What is the lingering effect on a Black woman's sense of herself based on [Black women's] particular history which distinguishes them from white women? How do Black women think of themselves as sexual beings" in light of the rape and abuse by white men during slavery and the shame that subsequently reverberates from that?[5] *Naked Acts* shows Cicely, who was sexually abused as a child, after she has lost fifty-seven pounds and now defies her mother's admonition to avoid a movie acting career. Although her mother was crudely used in 1970s blaxploitation films, Cicely is certain she can succeed differently until she too is asked to remove her clothes for a scene.

Davis studied film production in a year-long intensive program at New York's Third World Newsreel. She went to film panels and conferences and read everything she could find on the production, distribution, and marketing processes. Herman Lew, who taught her filmmaking, became her director of photography on *Naked Acts*. Her B.A. from Spelman, master's from Columbia, and experience as a journalist made it easier to research the film industry. Davis had no

BLACK WOMEN LOVE IT!

CROSSGRAIN PICTURES and RHINOCEROS PRODUCTIONS in Association With CHANNEL 4
Present A PARADISE PLUM Presentation of A Film By AYOKA CHENZIRA "ALMA'S RAINBOW"
Starring KIM WESTON-MORAN • VICTORIA GABRIELLA PLATT • MIZAN NUNES Music By LILLIAN BENSON
Editor Ronald K. Gray Camera SIDNEY KAI INNIS Designer THOMAS OSHA PINNOCK
Composer JEAN PAUL-BOURELLY Producer AYOKA CHENZIRA, HOWARD BRICKNER, CHARLES LANE
Written and Directed By AYOKA CHENZIRA

HEMDALE
COMMUNICATIONS, Inc.

Following successful engagements in
Chicago, Miami, Ohio, Philadelphia,
South Carolina, London, Milan, Los Angeles,

★ ★ ★ ★

The Newest Film By A Black Woman Director
Comes To Harlem

ALMA'S RAINBOW a film by AYOKA CHENZIRA

EXCLUSIVE ENGAGEMENT
Harlem Victoria V
235-237 West 125th Street / 212) 864-1900

SHOW TIMES: Monday through Thursday: 4, 6, 8
Friday through Sunday: 3:30, 5:30, 7:30, 9:30

"Sisters, take heart...we have been graced with "Alma's Rainbow...a sensually and spiritually stirring film"
The Other Paper, Ohio

"A hip urban sitcom..."
The New York Times

"...exotic spices in a steaming pot of bouillabaisse called "Alma's Rainbow"
South Carolina Post and Courier

"..... palpable smash hit female/rite-of-passage / romantic comedy drama ...a drop-dead triumph
Street News

"A lush vibrant film...You won't see a movie as witty and compelling as this one any time soon -- and you won't see one as beautiful."
Philadelphia City Paper

"Absorbed with femaleness, with class issues and maturity...the film is drenched in iridescent color, genuine humor and intimacy."
Philadelphia Welcome Mat

Flyer for Ayoka Chenzira's *Alma's Rainbow* (author's collection)

Naked Acts director Bridgett Davis and executive producer Henri Norris
(Jesse Rhines)

interest in Hollywood filmmaking, however. "Hollywood is a factory that mass produces films. I know about that. I grew up in Detroit. I never wanted to go to Hollywood. But I knew I had something important to say to a greater audience than I could reach as a journalist." She saved her earnings, cleaned up her credit rating, got a couple of new credit cards, and solicited small, incremental investments for a percentage of the box office return (points) to begin financing. In Detroit, Davis's sister, Rita, raised over $20,000 from family, relatives, and hometown friends as seed money during preproduction and early production. Her cast and crew, mostly people of color, some with industry experience, some without, worked based on Davis's expressed commitment to pay them when the film made money (deferral) in most cases. Davis ensured, however, that all technical people were paid up front. But her primary benefactor, Henri Norris, heard about the project through a friend

Winsome (Sandy Wilson), Cece (Jake-Ann Jones), and Dina (Reneé Cox)
in *Naked Acts* *(Donn Thompson, Photographer)*

who sent her a packet on it. She called Davis to say these body image issues were hers as well. Norris is a Black San Francisco activist attorney who has litigated multibillion-dollar product liability suits in class action cases like that concerning the Dalkon Shield. Now Norris, as *Naked Acts*'s executive producer, and Davis are in early negotiations with distributors.

Prospects for theatrical release for *Naked Acts* are not good because the elements of violence, sex, harrowing adventure, and comedy are not in the script. Yet *Daughters of the Dust* lacked these elements, and it went on to make a small profit. In addition, new venues emerge as the film industry's structure changes. Starting in the fall of 1994, *Filmmaker* magazine ran a series by Mary Glucksman on a new generation of distributors. From the independent producer's point of view the Big Six are formerly independent and boutique distributors Miramax, Fine Line, Gramercy, Goldwyn, Sony Classics, and October, which handle films in the $3 to $5 million range. For "no-budget" filmmakers like Bridgett Davis, there is an even newer crop of tiny distributors, changing almost day to day. Jonathan Dana, whose Triton distributed *American Heart*, *Hearts of Darkness*, *Mind Walk*, *A Brief History of Time*, and about fifteen additional titles, shut down in 1994. Dana says that "the market's in a state of turmoil. . . . The whole system's being co-opted by the studios. . . . [S]maller companies require more intense capitalization than ever."[6] Despite having made a profit on *Daughters of the Dust*, Kino International has not handled a fiction film since. Some of these tiny companies pick up a film only after a videotape distribution company has committed to release it. These "video dollars" are then used to finance marketing and print costs. A filmmaker may just have to wait until the film makes it or fails at the box office to get paid. He or she is likely to get no up-front money from a cash-poor distributor. "No-budget" films are being acquired, however. Savoy Pictures, which distributed *The Walking Dead*, picked up George Tilman's $150,000 feature *Scenes for the Soul* in early 1995.

There is even a glimmer of hope in Black distribution. In 1994 and 1995, *Sankofa*, written, directed, and produced by Ethiopian-born Haile Gerima, was distributed by Gerima's Mypheduh company and grossed more than $2.5 million. Gerima was at UCLA film

In *Sankofa,* three slaves who were running away are caught again
(Mypheduh Products/WDR)

school in the 1970s with Julie Dash and Charles Burnett. His feature films *Bush Mama, Harvest 2000,* and others have long been celebrated by Black intellectuals and film buffs, but *Sankofa* developed a large following in the mass Black population. Mypheduh normally distributes Gerima's films to libraries, universities, and limited theatrical engagement. U.S. distributors, considering *Sankofa* a "Black history" or "Black culture" film, turned it down, so Gerima "four-walled" it, as Melvin Van Peebles did *Sweetback* twenty years ago, by renting the Biograph Theater in Washington, D.C. To everyone's surprise, the seats remained packed by African Americans for eleven weeks. *Sankofa* has now played successfully in Newark, New Jersey, Los Angeles, and multiple venues in New York City. In New York, Mypheduh four-walled at the Thalia Theater for at least two six-month stints. In addition to Gerima's works, a series of other films considered "culturally authentic" to a large segment of the African American community were shown.

KJM3 has also remained active into 1995. Vice president Kathy

Bowser arranged *Sankofa*'s showings in Newark theaters. In mid-1995 they were involved in three projects. KJM3 entered a joint venture with the Black Entertainment Television cable channel to distribute *Out of Sync*, the film-directing debut of Debbie Allen, dancer and star of one of TV's longtime successes of the 1980s, *Fame*. They are also partnering with Miramax to distribute Charles Burnett's new feature, *Glass Shield*. KJM3 is also using an innovative approach to distributing the film *More Time*, which they bill as "a fresh and informative look at how issues of teen sexuality and AIDS are handled in contemporary southern Africa." With the objective of raising youth AIDS awareness, KJM3 invites corporations and community-oriented organizations to host one or two weeks of screenings in New York, Boston, Philadelphia, Washington, D.C., Chicago, Atlanta, Houston, or San Francisco. The one-time rental charge for the film plus *More Time* educational study guides is $500. KJM3 will then work with the sponsoring organization to develop fund-raising and publicity campaigns. The target audience for *More Time* is African American youths aged twelve to twenty-four. KJM3 says that this project's success will "lay the foundation for introducing similar positive film works to this target audience and provide a continuous platform for [the sponsor's] community outreach efforts."[7]

As the 1990s progress, then, African Americans, though still very much at the margins, continue to make both Hollywood and independent feature films. Their entrepreneurial presence behind the camera expands in a number of venues, including publicity, casting, and distribution. The progress on non-Black production, however, has contracted. Although Alan Dinwiddie has moved from vice president of special marketing to a position of greater influence at Disney, *Variety* reports work is still scarce for minorities despite concerted efforts by the craft unions. In 1994, the DGA said, "Our initial report two years ago demonstrated that the goal of a level playing field for women and minorities was nowhere in sight from 1983 through 1991 . . . Over the past two years, that situation has not improved, and for some categories employment opportunities are below the previous level." The 4 percent of all guild days worked by minorities in 1993 was a drop from 5 percent in 1983. For second

Brooklyn high school students Tahisha Beresford (*holding microphone*) and Amoura Bryan paid $25 each to attend Spike Lee's seminar "A Director's Perspective on Filmmaking" in February 1994 *(Jesse Rhines)*

assistant directors, the drop was from 17 percent to 10 percent. DGA executive director Glenn Gumpel said that both minorities and women "appear to be barely holding on to previous gains."[8]

African American filmmakers like Spike Lee continue to encourage youths to perfect their craft. For the past five years Lee has hosted a public film craft "teach-in" at the Brooklyn campus of Long Island University near Fort Greene. Topics for these seminars have included "Breaking into the Film Industry," "The Music Video Industry," "Working Music in Films," and "The Art of Screenwriting." The cost is twenty-five dollars per person, and anyone may attend. On February 5, 1995, Lee himself made a presentation to an audience of about three hundred people. I happened to sit with two high school students, ninth-grader Tahisha and tenth-grader Amoura, who were thrilled at the thought of seeing and talking with Spike Lee. A 150-page booklet entitled "A Director's Perspective on Filmmaking" had been passed out, and the girls thumbed through it as they asked me questions about both college and the film industry. This booklet included excerpts from Lee's scripts and sample story boards. The session was interactive, with Lee referring to the booklet, answering questions, and passing around the original story board for one of his films, saying to the audience, "This is my only copy. Now y'all take care of it and make sure I get it back." I gave Tahisha and Amoura the picture of Lee included in my press packet, and they passed this photograph back and forth throughout the event. These young women had planned for this day. They had sacrificed and saved their money to attend this seminar. Clearly they perceived this as an important opportunity, and since that time I have advised them on chosing a college. There is no doubt that the new Black filmmakers are a source of inspiration for African Americans unsure as to how to build their futures.

Notes

Introduction

1. "The Faltering Dream," *The Cronkite Report #3,* Cronkite-Ward Productions, Discovery Channel, Monday, October 18, 1993.

2. John Izod, *Hollywood and the Box Office* (New York: Columbia University Press, 1988), p. xi.

3. "Out of Focus—Out of Sync (A Report on the Film and Television Industries)," NAACP Economic Development Department, September 3, 1991, p. 3.

4. Ayoka Chenzira interview, June 3, 1994.

Chapter 1   Distribution, Production, and Exhibition

1. Suzanne Mary Donahue, *American Film Distribution* (Ann Arbor: UMI Research Press, 1987), p. 35.

2. Gary R. Edgerton, *American Film Exhibition* (New York: Garland Publishing, 1983), p. 11.

3. Ibid., pp. 10, 12, 14.

4. David F. Prindle, *Risky Business: The Political Economy of Hollywood* (San Francisco: Westview Press, 1993), pp. 35–39.

5. James Monaco, *American Film Now,* 2d ed. (New York: Zoetrope, 1984), p. 44.

6. Garth Jowett and James M. Linton, *Movies as Mass Communication,* 2d ed. (London: Sage Publications, 1989), p. 45.

7. Donahue, *Distribution,* p. 105.

8. Edgerton, *Exhibition,* p. 72.

9. Ibid., p. 74.

10. Jowett and Linton, *Communication,* p. 39.

11. "Hollywood Prod. Labor in a Boom Season," *Variety,* December 28, 1983, p. 3.

Chapter 2   The Silent Era

1. James R. Nesteby, *Black Images in American Films, 1896–1954* (Lanham, Md.: University Press of America), p. 65.

2. Thomas Cripps, *Slow Fade to Black* (New York: Oxford University Press, 1977), p. 12.

3. Donald Bogle, *Toms, Coons, Mulattoes, Mammies, and Bucks* (New York: Continuum, 1991), p. 7.

4. James A. Snead, "Images of Blacks in Black Independent Films: A Brief Survey," in Mbye B. Cham and Claire Andrade-Watkins, eds., *Blackframes* (Cambridge: MIT Press, 1988), p. 16.

5. W.E.B. Du Bois, *Dusk at Dawn* (New York: Harcourt, Brace, [c.1940]), p. 235.

6. Maxim Simcovitch, "The Impact of Griffith's *Birth of a Nation* on the Modern Ku Klux Klan," in David Platt, ed., *Celluloid Power* (Metuchen, N.J.: Scarecrow Press, 1992), p. 76.

7. Sumiko Higashi, "Ethnicity, Class, and Gender in Film: DeMille's *The Cheat*," in Lester D. Friedman, ed., *Unspeakable Images* (Urbana: University of Illinois Press, 1991), p. 121.

8. Cripps, *Slow Fade,* p. 37.

9. Quoted in Michael Paul Rogin, "'The Sword Became a Flashing Vision': D. W. Griffith's *The Birth of a Nation,*" in *Ronald Reagan, the Movie, and Other Episodes in Political Demonology* (Berkeley and Los Angeles: University of California Press, 1987), p. 219.

10. Neal Gabler, *An Empire of Their Own: How the Jews Invented Hollywood* (New York: Crown Publishers, 1988), p. 90.

11. Ibid., p. 91.

12. For more on this conflict see Louis R. Harlin, "Booker T. Washington and the Politics of Accommodation," and Elliott Rudwick, "W.E.B. Du Bois: Protagonist of the Afro-American Protest," in John Hope Franklin and August Meier, eds., *Black Leaders of the Twentieth Century* (Urbana: University of Illinois Press, 1982).

13. John Brown Childs, *Leadership, Conflict, and Cooperation in Afro-American Social Thought* (Philadelphia: Temple University Press, 1989), p. 39.

14. Cripps, *Slow Fade,* p. 70.

15. Ibid., pp. 70, 71.

16. Gabler, *Empire,* p. 59.

17. Ibid., p. 64.

18. Cripps, *Slow Fade,* p. 72.

19. Ibid, pp. 74–75.

20. Snead, "Images of Blacks," p. 18.

21. Cripps, *Slow Fade,* p. 78.

22. Nesteby, *Black Images,* p. 69.

23. Cripps, *Slow Fade,* p. 79.

24. George Johnson kept a file with news clippings, advertising brochures, and business plans for all the Black motion picture companies he encountered. That file is currently a part of the archival collection at UCLA.

25. Cripps, *Slow Fade,* p. 80.

26. Ibid., pp. 153, 82.

27. Gabler, *Empire*, p. 48.

28. Nesteby, *Black Images*, p. 69.

29. James Murray, *To Find an Image* (New York: Bobbs-Merrill, 1973), p. 8.

30. Ibid., p. 9.

31. Nesteby, *Black Images*, p. 75.

32. Ibid., p. 76.

33. Bogle, *Toms*, p. 110.

Chapter 3   Depression and World War II

1. Ronald Takaki, *A Different Mirror* (Boston: Little, Brown, 1993), p. 366.

2. Ibid.

3. Dona Cooper Hamilton and Charles V. Hamilton, "The Dual Agenda of African American Organizations since the New Deal: Social Welfare Policies and Civil Rights," *Political Science Quarterly* 107, no. 3 (1992): 440.

4. Ibid., p. 441. Italics in the original.

5. Edward Peeks, *The Long Struggle for Black Power* (New York: Scribner's, 1971), p. 231.

6. Ibid., p. 233.

7. Takaki, *A Different Mirror*, pp. 368–369.

8. Ibid., p. 369.

9. Mark Reid, *Redefining Black Film* (Berkeley and Los Angeles: University of California Press, 1993), p. 16.

10. Cripps, *Slow Fade*, p. 220.

11. Bogle, *Toms*, p. 118.

12. Ed Guerrero, *Framing Blackness* (Philadelphia: Temple University Press, 1993), p. 24.

13. See Bogle, *Toms*, for detailed information on these stereotypes.

14. Cripps, *Slow Fade*, pp. 220–221.

15. Nesteby, *Black Images*, pp. 78–79.

16. Murray, *Find an Image*, p. 12.

17. Nesteby, *Black Images*, p. 89.

18. Murray, *Find an Image*, pp. 12–13.

19. Snead, "Images of Blacks," p. 21.

Chapter 4   The Negro Cycle through Blaxploitation

1. Takaki, *A Different Mirror*, pp. 396–397.

2. Ibid.

3. Paul Gordon Lauren, *Power and Prejudice* (Boulder: Westview Press, 1988), p. 141.

4. Ibid., p. 160.

5. Takaki, *A Different Mirror,* p. 399.

6. Nesteby, *Black Images,* p. 249.

7. Takaki, *A Different Mirror,* p. 404.

8. Thomas Cripps, *Making Movies Black* (New York: Oxford University Press, 1993), p. 291.

9. Murray, *Find an Image,* p. 65.

10. See Stokely Carmichael, "A Declaration of War," in Mitchell Goodman, ed., *The Movement toward A New America* (New York: Knopf, 1970), pp. 180–185, and Stokely Carmichael and Charles V. Hamilton, *Black Power* (New York: Vintage Books, 1967).

11. Raymond L. Hall, *Black Separatism in the United States* (Hanover, N.H.: University Press of New England, 1978), p. 116.

12. Ibid., p. 113.

13. "The Time Has Come," *Eyes on the Prize,* film documentary, Blackside Productions, 1990.

14. Murray, *Find an Image,* p. 73.

15. Guerrero, *Framing,* p. 86.

16. Charles P. Henry, *Culture and African American Politics* (Bloomington: Indiana University Press, 1990), p. 93.

17. Nelson George, *Blackface* (New York: HarperCollins, 1994), p. 54.

18. Bogle, *Toms,* p. 242.

19. Ibid.

20. Murray, *Find an Image,* p. 84.

21. Ibid., p. 89.

22. Ibid., p. 134.

23. Barbara Campbell, "Third World Pins Movie Hopes on *Claudine* Run," *New York Times,* June 5, 1975, p. 49.

24. Murray, *Find an Image,* p. 112.

25. Ibid.

26. Ibid., p. 125.

27. Ibid., p. 123.

Chapter 5   Blockbusters and Independents

1. Jowett and Linton, *Communication,* p. 35.

2. Donahue, *Distribution,* p. 103.

3. Jowett and Linton, *Communication,* p. 34.

4. Guerrero, *Framing,* p. 70.

5. Monaco, *Film Now,* p. 25.

6. Ibid.

7. Edgerton, *Exhibition,* p. 55.

8. Clint C. Wilson II and Felix Gutierrez, *Minorities and Media* (Beverly Hills: Sage Publications, 1985), pp. 54–55.

9. Ibid., p. 40.

10. Izod, *Box Office,* p. 181.

11. Michael Dempsey and Udayan Gupta, "Hollywood's Color Problem," *American Film* 7, no. 6 (April 1982): 68.

12. Janet Wasko, *Movies and Money* (Norwood, Conn.: Ablex Publishing, 1982), p. xix; Monaco, *Film Now,* p. 22.

13. Jowett and Linton, *Communication,* pp. 26, 30.

14. Donahue, *Distribution,* p. 83.

15. Ibid., p. 58.

16. Ibid., p. 73.

17. CNN's *Inside Business,* aired in New York on March 29, 1993, featured Home Box Office, *Variety,* and National Westminister Bank executives who spoke to this issue.

18. Spike Lee, "Class Act," *American Film* 13, no. 3 (January/February 1988): 57.

19. Monona Wali, "LA Black Filmmakers Thrive Despite Hollywood's Monopoly," *Black Film Review* 2, no. 2 (Spring 1986): 10.

20. J. Hoberman, "The Non-Hollywood Hustle," *American Film* 6, no. 1 (October 1980): 54–55.

21. Lee, "Class Act," 57.

22. Trey Ellis, "The New Black Aesthetic," *Callaloo* 12, no. 1 (Winter 1989): 237.

23. Interview with an Island Pictures executive, November 10, 1992.

24. Letter from an Island Pictures executive, March 11, 1994.

25. Dennis Greene interview, October 5, 1992.

26. Amy Dawes, "Time to 'Party' for Hudlins; Brothers Ink Film, TV Deals," *Variety,* June 27, 1990, p. 16.

27. Jacqueline Bobo, "Conference Report," *Available Visions: Improving Distribution of African American Independent Film and Video Conference, July 24–26, 1992,* San Francisco Arts Commission, December 1992, p. 11.

28. Interview with a group of KJM3 vice presidents, October 1, 1992.

29. Ibid.

30. Talmadge Anderson, *Introduction to African American Studies* (Dubuque: Kendall/Hunt, 1993), p. 252.

31. KJM3 vice presidents interview.

32. Bobo, "Conference Report," p. 15.

33. While use of the term *authentic* to delineate a cultural tradition has recently come under question, KJM3's usage reflects that of philosopher Jean-Paul Sartre. Sartre said of the European Jew within a context dominated by gentiles: "What the least favored of men ordinarily discover in their situation is a bond of concrete solidarity with other men . . . The sole tie that binds them is the hostility and disdain of the societies which surround them. Thus the authentic Jew is the one who asserts his claim in the face of the disdain shown toward him." Jean-Paul Sartre, *Anti-Semite and Jew* (New York: Schocken Books, 1976), p. 91.

34. KJM3 Entertainment Group, Inc., brochure acquired April 1995.

35. KJM3 vice presidents interview.

36. Bobo, "Conference Report," p. 14.

37. Ibid., p. 15.

38. Kenneth Turan, "*Boomerang*: Eddie Murphy's Romantic Fling," *Los Angeles Times,* July 1, 1991, p. F1.

39. Izod, *Box Office,* p. 172.

40. Although theater attendance for *Boomerang* was less than projected, Warrington Hudlin, the film's producer, says it was the number one grosser three weeks running upon its videocassette release.

41. Spike Lee interview.

42. Turan, "Romantic Fling," p. F7.

43. Delvin Molden, *African American Film Statistics and Marketing Strategies* (Chicago: D. Molden, 1994), n.p.; Jan Hoffman, "Mom Always Said, Don't Take the First $2 Million Offer," *New York Times,* October 9, 1994, p. H28.

44. Spike Lee interview.

45. Andy Meisler, "Using Fun to Show Blacks to Whites," *New York Times,* November 7, 1994.

Chapter 6   Employment Discrimination

1. Wilson and Gutierrez, *Minorities and Media,* p. 156.

2. Ibid., p. 157.

3. Ibid.

4. "SAG Seeks 40% Wage Hike, Profit Share, Affirmative Action," *Variety,* June 4, 1980, pp. 3, 26.

5. Jim Robbins, "Theme of Newark's Black Fest: Hollywood Mostly Cold to Race," *Variety,* June 16, 1982, pp. 6, 22.

6. "NAACP Puts Aside Film Boycott Threat after Studio Summit," *Variety,* January 13, 1982, p. 7.

7. Will Tusher, "Next NAACP/Studio Meet Mulls Black Share of Pic Audience," *Variety,* January 20, 1982, p. 5.

8. Will Tusher, "NAACP Seeks Logo-by-Logo Data, Rejects MPAA Facts as Vague; Possible Boycott Come April," *Variety,* February 24, 1982, p. 4.

9. "NAACP to Target One Major Studio for 'Direct Action,'" *Variety*, August 11, 1982, p. 37.

10. Dempsey and Gupta, "Hollywood's Color Problem," p. 2.

11. "Who's Who of Companies, Guilds Set for 1st Minorities Hearing," *Variety*, September 15, 1982, pp. 7, 37.

12. Lawrence Cohn, "Black Pic Employment Still Lags," *Variety*, December 1, 1982, p. 1.

13. "Black Pic Outlook Dark," *Variety*, December 1, 1982, p. 32.

14. David Robb, "MGM/UA Sign with NAACP to Expand Overall Black Presence," *Variety*, December 29, 1982, p. 3.

15. David Robb, "Breakdown of Hollywood Minority Hiring," *Variety*, April 13, 1983, p. 5.

16. "Casting Report by SAG Shows Minorities Lose," *Variety*, April 13, 1983, p. 1.

17. David Robb, "DGA Gets EEOC Nod to File Class-Action Discrimination Suit against Webs, Majors, Indies," *Variety*, May 18, 1983, p. 4.

18. "Directors Guild Is Pushing Producers over Minority Hiring," *Variety*, June 1, 1983, p. 3.

19. "Two Blacks Quit SAG-Committee over Issues of 'Numerical Goals,'" *Variety*, April 20, 1983, p. 22.

20. "DGA Hits Warners with 'Discriminatory Hiring' Class Action, *Variety*, July 27, 1983, p. 3.

21. "Boon to Columbia as Marketing Chief in Antonnowsky Job," *Variety*, November 16, 1983, pp. 3, 17.

22. David Robb, "DGA and Columbia Lock Horns over Affirmative Action," *Variety*, November 9, 1983, p. 22.

23. "Columbia May Countersue DGA over Discriminatory Hiring Claim," *Variety*, November 16, 1983, p. 25.

24. David Robb, "Casting Report by SAG Shows Minorities Lose," *Variety*, April 6, 1983, p. 1.

25. "Study Sees Bias Favoring White Male Writers," *Variety*, June 24, 1987, p. 1.

26. Dempsey and Gupta, "Hollywood's Color Problem," p. 69.

27. David Nicholson, "The Great Black Hope," *Black Film Review* 2, no. 3 (Summer 1986): 30.

28. "The Best in the Business," *Jade* 1, no. 3 (Spring 1975): 9.

29. Chris Hodenfield, "To Market, To Market . . . ," *American Film* 14, no. 9 (July/August 1989): 2.

30. Joy Horowitz, "Hollywood's Dirty Little Secret," *Premiere*, March 1989, p. 58.

31. Robert W. Welkos, "Minorities Still Largely Shut Out of Film Studios' Executive Posts," *Daily Californian* (Berkeley), September 3, 1992, p. 13.

32. Thomas R. King, "Cut! Hollywood's Budget-mindedness Sets Black Filmmakers Back Again," *Wall Street Journal*, February 19, 1993, p. R12.

33. Deborah Orr, "Blacks Who Won't Do the White Thing," *Guardian* (Manchester, N.H.), September 10, 1991, p. 34.

Chapter 7   Black Women in the System

1. Yvonne Welbon, "Calling the Shots: Black Women Directors Take the Helm," *Independent,* March 1992, pp. 18–22.

2. Unless otherwise noted, Janet Grillo quotations are taken from an interview with the author, November 11, 1992.

3. Interview with source at New Line, September 12, 1995.

4. Letter from Janet Grillo, March 5, 1994.

5. Interview with a Gramercy Pictures executive, November 10, 1992.

6. Welbon, "Calling the Shots," p. 18.

7. Ibid., p. 19.

8. Julie Dash, *Daughters of the Dust* (New York: New Press, 1992), pp. 7–8.

9. Ibid., p. 10. Dash refers to "Women Make Movies Too" and "Appalshop, Southeast Regional Fellowship"; my adjustments to these organizations' names are based on telephone conversations with their representatives, September 12, 1995.

10. Ibid., p. 25.

11. Ibid., p. 26.

12. Ibid., p. 40.

13. Robin Downes quotations are taken from an interview with the author, September 28, 1992.

14. Monica Breckenridge quotations are taken from an interview with the author, January 15, 1993.

15. Donna Daniels, press packet for *Just Another Girl on the IRT* (1992), pp. 1–4.

16. Bernard Weinraub, "A Trip Straight Out of Brooklyn to the Sundance Film Festival," *New York Times,* January 26, 1993, p. C11.

Chapter 8   Unintended Collusion

1. Ellis, "New Black Aesthetic," pp. 239–242.

2. Warrington Hudlin, "BFF Turns 10," *Black Face* 1, no. 1 (Fall 1989): 9.

3. David Nicholson, "Which Way the Black Film Movement?" *Black Film Review* 5, no. 2 (Spring 1989): p. 17.

4. *Cinéaste* is defined in one French dictionary as "collaborateur technique du cinéma." *Larousse de Pouche* (New York: Washington Square Press, 1974), p. 69.

5. For a critique of gender aspects of this film see Julianne Malveaux, "Spike's Spite: Women at the Periphery," *Women's Resource Center Newsletter* (University of California at San Francisco) 5, no. 19 (December 1991–February 1992): 1.

6. It is interesting to note in this regard that Lee has had an ongoing dispute with Amiri Baraka, one of the best-known enunciators of a Black cultural national identity in the 1970s.

7. *Primetime Live,* ABC News, August 2, 1990.

8. Jerome Christensen, "Spike Lee, Corporate Populist," *Critical Inquiry* 17 (Spring 1991): 588–589.

9. Pete Hamill, "American Journal," *Esquire,* August 1991, p. 26.

10. Mark Landler, "Spike Lee Does a Lot of Things Right," *Business Week,* August 6, 1990, p. 62.

11. Pauline Kael, "The Current Cinema: Bodies," *New Yorker,* October 6, 1986, p. 127.

12. Stanley Kauffman, "Stanley Kauffman on Films: New Women," *New Republic,* September 15–22, 1986, p. 30.

13. D. Denby, "Movies: Roughing It," *New York,* August 18, 1986, p. 59.

14. Stuart Mieher, "Spike Lee's Gotta Have It," *New York Times Magazine,* August 9, 1987, p. 26.

15. Jack Barth, "Spike Lee on Deck," *Village Voice,* August 12, 1986, p. 56.

16. The evolution of concern over the development of two distinct Black urban socioeconomic classes is clearly seen in the increasing scholarly and popular use of the term *underclass* as the 1980s progressed. The *Reader's Guide to Periodical Literature* indexes popular publications such as *Time* and *Newsweek* magazines as well as more scholarly journals such as *The Progressive* and *World Press Review.* Growth in popular publications' use of the term *underclass* in article titles is evident. In 1983, the word *underclass* appeared five times; in 1986, it appeared seven times. In 1988, there were nineteen uses of the term, largely as a result of popular reviews and commentary on W. J. Wilson's 1987 book *The Truly Disadvantaged,* but usage dropped back to twelve in 1992. In addition, *underclass* was not listed as an index category in the *Reader's Guide* until 1986, when it guided the reader to "See *poor*" but had no listings of its own. In 1988, *underclass* was a category unto itself complete with its own listings and without reference to "poor." This growth of the popular use of the term *underclass* reflected white America's increasing concern—particularly in light of the twenty-fifth anniversary of the Kerner Commission Report—with the unexpectedly large number of Blacks who not only had not benefited from the civil rights movement in any tangible way but were actually becoming worse off relative to whites.

17. William J. Wilson, *The Truly Disadvantaged* (Chicago: University of Chicago Press, 1987), p. 8.

18. William Julius Wilson, *The Declining Significance of Race* (Chicago: University of Chicago Press, 1978), p. 209, n. 22.

19. "How Right Is *Do the Right Thing?*" *Nightline,* ABC News, July 6, 1989, transcript, p. 2.

20. Ibid., p. 3.

21. Mieher, "Lee's Gotta Have It," p. 39.

22. Jacquie Jones, "Spike Lee's Look at the Realities of Racism," *Black Film Review* 5, no. 2 (Spring 1989): 13.

23. Ibid.

24. *Nightline,* July 6, 1989, p. 4.

25. "Black in White America," *Nightline,* ABC News, August 29, 1989, transcript, p. 6.

26. Spike Lee interview.

27. Spike Lee, "Top Spin," *Spin* 6, no. 7 (October 1990): 8.

28. Spike Lee, "Eddie," ibid., p. 36.

29. Spike Lee, "The Gospel According to Reverend Al," ibid., p. 92.

30. Michel Foucault, *Discipline and Punish* (New York: Vintage Books, 1979), p. 170.

31. Gerald David Jaynes and Robert M. Williams Jr., eds., *A Common Destiny: Blacks and American Society* (Washington, D.C.: National Academy Press, 1989), p. 22.

32. Ronald Takaki, "Race as a Site of Discipline and Punish," unpublished monograph, University of California, Berkeley, 1993, p. 15.

33. Wilson, *Disadvantaged,* p. 33.

34. Ibid., p. 34.

35. Spike Lee interview.

36. Jaynes and Williams, *Common Destiny,* p. 320.

37. Ronald Takaki, *Iron Cages* (Oxford: Oxford University Press, 1990), p. 295.

38. Spike Lee interview.

39. Spike Lee, *Spike Lee's Gotta Have It* (New York: Fireside, 1987), p. 325.

40. Robert Chrisman, "What Is the Right Thing? Notes on the Deconstruction of Black Ideology," *Black Scholar* 21, no. 2 (May 1990): 53.

41. J. Hoberman, "Pass/Fail," *Village Voice,* July 11, 1989, p. 59.

42. Sheila Benson, *Los Angeles Times,* Calendar, June 30, 1989.

43. Vincent Canby, "Spike Lee Tackles Racism in *Do the Right Thing,*" *New York Times,* June 30, 1989.

44. Shelby Steele, *The Content of Our Character* (New York: Harper Perennial, 1991), p. 95.

45. Ronald Takaki, "A Dream Deferred: The Crisis of 'Losing Ground,'" in Ronald Takaki, ed., *From Different Shores* (New York: Oxford University Press, 1987), p. 248.

46. Spike Lee interview.

47. Ibid.

48. Spike Lee with Lisa Jones, *The Construction of School Daze* (New York: Fireside, 1988), p. 121.

49. Spike Lee interview.

50. Linda Hutcheon, *The Politics of Postmodernism* (New York: Routledge, 1989), p. 4.

51. Lee, *Construction of School Daze,* p. 15.

52. Spike Lee interview.

53. Stanley Nelson interview, October 5, 1992.

54. Anderson, *African American Studies,* pp. 251–252.

55. Reginald Hudlin interview, March 10, 1993.

Chapter 9   The Struggle Continues

1. Jaynes and Williams, *Common Destiny,* p. 43.

2. Grace Blake quotations are taken from an interview with the author, March 30, 1993.

3. Murray, *Find an Image,* p. 64.

4. Reginald Hudlin interview.

5. I was in the Yale Summer High School one year before Warrington. Shelby Steele, a scholar and political neoconservative whose individualistic, "bootstrapping" development philosophy is distinct from that offered by William Julius Wilson, was Warrington's mentor in the Dunham program.

6. Spike Lee interview.

7. Cliff Frazier quotations are taken from an interview with the author, April 19, 1993.

8. Michael Fleming, "Blacks See Red over Lily-white Film Crews," *Variety,* October 14, 1991, pp. 1, 261.

9. Michael Fleming, "N.Y. Panel Offers Plan to Integrate Crews," *Variety,* March 2, 1992, p. 8.

10. Telephone conversation with Patricia Reed Scott, commissioner of the Mayor's Office on Film, Theatre, and Broadcasting, September 18, 1995.

11. Fleming, "Blacks See Red," p. 261.

12. Reginald Hudlin interview.

13. *Future Directions,* conference report, "Reunion 2000," International Communications Association, Inc., Kaufman Astoria Studio, Astoria, New York, September 1992, pp. 9, 16.

Conclusion

1. Gary Crowdus and Dan Georgakas, "Our Film Is Only a Starting Point: An Interview with Spike Lee," *Cineaste* 19, no. 3 and no. 4 (March 1993): 20.

2. Todd Boyd, "Popular Culture and Political Empowerment: The Americanization and Death of Malcolm X," *Cineaste* 19, no. 3 and no. 4 (March 1993): 13.

3. Manning Marable, "Malcolm as Messiah: Cultural Myth vs. Historical Reality in *Malcolm X,*" *Cineaste* 19, no. 3 and no. 4 (March 1993): 8.

4. Conference flyer, in author's possession.

Epilogue

1. George T. Chronis, "Projecting Past the Millennium," *Boxoffice,* June 1992, p. 32.

2. Evette Porter, "Black Marketing," *Village Voice,* September 13, 1994, p. 68.

3. Dennis Greene, "Tragically Hip," *Cineaste* 20, no. 4 (October 1994): 28.

4. Terrence Dixon, "*The Walking Dead* Rests Asleep on the Screen," *Rutgers Observer,* March 7, 1995.

5. Bridgett Davis quotations are taken from an interview with the author, February 19, 1995.

6. Mary Glucksman, "The State of Things," *Filmmaker* (Fall 1994): 24.

7. KJM3 brochure on *More Time,* in author's possession.

8. Dan Cox, "Work Still Scarce for Most Women, Minority Helmers," *Variety,* May 30, 1994, p. 7.

Index

ABC News, on Spike Lee, 107, 110–112

affirmative action: Reginald Hudlin on, 146; litigation, 79–82; and new Black filmmakers, 104

African Americans: continuing struggle of, 104; film industry employment of, 87, 146; 1970s new attitude of, 43; prison statistics on, 118

African American women: Julie Dash on, 97; directors, versus distributors, 96; financial viability of their stories, 96; lack of directoral success of, 88; Charles Murray on financial dependence of, 126

Allen, Debbie, 173

Alma's Rainbow (Chenzira), 7, 167

Amblin Entertainment, 8

Amergro Films, 35

American Film Institute, 88, 101, 142

"Anatomy of an Industry" conference, 160

anti-trust, 2. *See also* Paramount Consent Decree

art: in African cultures, 133; authentic Black, 65; as commodity, 55; as filmmaker's goal, 5; films, 58–60; for art's sake, 103; and Spike Lee, 108, 130; and Oscar Micheaux, 24; programs, 140; racial uplift, and financial success, 103

Asians: acceptance by whites, 6; concentration of in central cities, 119; as depicted in white films, 17

audience: Black percentage of, 7; for Black underclass images, 110, 123; for blaxploitation films, 45; for *Daughters of the Dust*, 98; and distribution fees, 9; for Goldberg brothers' films, 35; and Lincoln Pictures, 22; mainstream, 8; mass, 53–60, 161; for Oscar Micheaux's films, 25; post–World War II, 40; and segregation, 15; for *She's Gotta Have*

It, 62–74; and sound synchronization, 31; white, for Spike Lee, 107, 108; for white films about Blacks, 163

authentically Black: as defined by KJM3, 65, 68, 69; Haile Gerima as, 172

"B" movies, 10, 76

"bad Nigger," 42–44

Barbour, Julia, vii

Beat Street (Lathan), 50

Bebe's Kids (Hudlin brothers), 76

Belafonte, Harry, 40, 46, 48, 49, 150

Berry, John, 47

Birth of a Nation, The (Griffith), 2, 15–20, 23, 25

Birth of a Race, The (Du Bois/ Washington), 17, 19, 20, 21, 103

Blacks: class bifurcation of, 110; cultural character as distinguishable from whites, 106; filmmakers, as exploited cheap labor, 77. *See also* African Americans

Black Filmmaker Foundation, 60, 61; creation of, 104

Blake, Grace, 91, 138–140, 144, 146, 147, 158

blaxploitation, 4, 17, 36, 40, 43–46, 51, 62, 70, 77, 88, 152, 167

blind bidding, 10

blockbusters, 1, 51, 53–56, 58, 64, 76, 77, 162

Blood of Jesus, The (Williams), 35

Body and Soul (Micheaux), 24, 25

Boomerang (Hudlin brothers), 68, 69, 71, 74, 76, 77, 93, 140, 146, 147

boycotts, 79–81

Boyz N the Hood (Singleton), 70, 75, 157

Brecher, Leo, and Frank Schiffman, 31

Breckenridge, Monica, 100, 102

Brotherhood of Sleeping Car Porters, 37

Bright Road (Gerald Mayer), 40

Brooks, Clarence, 21

About the Author

Jesse Algeron Rhines is an assistant professor of political economy in the African American and African Studies Department at Rutgers University, Newark, New Jersey. He is assistant editor of *Cineaste* magazine and coeditor of the magazine's regular "Race in Contemporary American Cinema" section. Dr. Rhines has worked as an IBM systems engineer, a janitor (twice), and on both congressional and mayoral staffs. A native of Washington, D.C., Dr. Rhines now lives in New York City. He received his B.A. in political communications from Antioch University, an M.A. in African American studies from Yale University, an M.A. in political science from UCLA, a certificate in film production from NYU, and his doctorate in ethnic studies from the University of California at Berkeley.